THE SIMPLE TRUTH
ABOUT WESTERN
LAND INVESTMENT

The Simple Truth about Western Land Investment

Leland Frederick Cooley
and
Lee Morrison Cooley

Drawings by Ed Nofziger

Doubleday & Company, Inc.
Garden City, New York

*This book is dedicated to old friends and
neighbors in Southern California's fabulous
Antelope Valley and to new friends in Florida,
New York State, Hawaii, Arizona and Nevada who
helped us prove that fine opportunities await
the modest land investor in all of our states.*

It is a very comfortable thing
to stand on your own ground.
Land is the only thing
that can't fly away.

Anthony Trollope

CONTENTS

Introduction

"WESTWARD WHOA!"

Trying to stop the present runaway migration to the western region of the United States is like trying to stem an avalanche. Within the last year several scholarly books have been written which explain, in part at least, the reasons for this great national movement. They seem to be three-fold; a desire to live in the equable climate along the Pacific coastal shelf, an area many GI's discovered during the late war and determined to return to with their families; a need to escape from present cramped living in congested eastern cities; and, most important, the need for still more space in which to accommodate the thousands of new-born Americans that swell our census rolls by nearly 9000 infant citizens per day.

This, of course, is an oversimplification of an extremely complex problem, one that is engaging more and more of the attention of sociologists and economists all over the land. And well it might since some startling new research indicates that by the year 2000 we Americans may be in short supply of almost everything but *people* unless we accelerate our long-range urban, suburban, industrial, agricultural, and recreational planning.

Approximately half of the land in the eleven western states is government-owned or controlled. The habitable portions of the remaining half are filling with new population so rapidly that the Pacific coastal shelf is already burdened and it is hardly an exaggeration to say that, for all practical purposes, it is "settled" from the Mexican border to the Canadian border.

The population density is not uniform in the areas between

the metropolitan centers of San Diego, Los Angeles, Santa Barbara, San Francisco, Portland, and Seattle. There are still vast areas of unsettled or unsettle-able land along the coast, effectively debarring urban development because they are devoted to military reservations, great private land holdings, national forests, or state parks. The result has been a "back pressure" of people which has forced population into the interior valleys and even into adjacent states.

This pressure, the main force of which we have named "people pressure," has had effects both salutory and sad upon western land. On the positive side it has brought in some areas increases in value far beyond the most extravagant predictions of the pioneer visionaries. On the other hand, exploited by a noisy minority of unscrupulous land promoters, the demand for a piece of "rapidly disappearing" western land has led to some of the most outrageous land swindles in the history of our country.

This book has no purpose other than to attempt to take an objective look at western land in terms of its suitability as an investment or a speculation. *It does not mean to recommend or favor one area of the west over another.*

We have used as examples of our own method for finding suitable investment land those areas with which we are the most familiar and can, therefore, speak about with the most authority. This does not infer that the opportunities there are necessarily any more desirable than in comparable areas of other states.

As a matter of fact, excluding the coastal plain, it is accurate to say that the rest of the west—on to the Rocky Mountains and even a bit beyond—is "all of a piece" geologically, sociologically, and economically. Geological purists may, with some justice, argue that point, but most geographers won't.

Between the Sierra Nevada and the Rockies we have traveled the Great Basin from border to border. In every state we have come upon areas in which we would like to live awhile. More than once on this most recent 7000-mile research trip, we would pull our road weary buggy off to the side, look out upon a breath-taking piece of scenery, and say, "Wouldn't it be wonderful if we could take a magic pill and live to be Methuselahs so we could really reside awhile in each of these beautiful places?"

The places ranged from the Jackson Hole Country in Wyoming to Salt Lake City, to Flathead Lake and Coeur D'Alene, to Lake Tahoe and the Reno-Carson City area, to Las Vegas, to Phoenix and Tucson, to Denver and Colorado Springs and Estes Park, to Albuquerque, to Lakes Mead, Mohave, and Havasu, and to the Salton Sea, just to name a few. In character they range from high mountain resorts to low desert retreats and everywhere we found spectacular beauty and the friendliest, most thoughtful people we've met anywhere in the world.

Our West is the land of America's legendry. It is the crucible in which was tempered our national conviction that we are, individually and collectively, the strongest, richest, freest, and most blessed people on earth. We can't imagine an American traveling through this magnificent land of our last frontier without responding to it and pausing, however briefly, to give thanks that during his lifetime he can be a custodian of a portion of it and is, as a citizen, a trustee of all of it.

This book is the story of how we became custodians not of one but several parcels of western land and how, in the process, we not only came to know our country and its people far better than we had but how we also achieved another great satisfaction, that of securing our own future well being.

We feel that any person of average intelligence and means can do the same thing. In fact, many of our friends have taken their first adventurous steps because they have seen how simple the process is once its basic rules are understood.

When one writes an instructive book—a "how-to" book as they are often termed—one is supposed to make the process of learning sound *ridiculously* easy.

So deeply ingrained is this "something for nothing" philosophy in many Americans these days that one of the all-time hits of the Broadway season is a musical which points a satirical finger at it. The show is, *How to Succeed in Business without Really Trying.*

Nothing worthwhile is ever accomplished without really trying. The more you put into an effort the more you get out of it—and not the least of the rewards is the satisfaction of knowing that you've done a good job of work.

Just a little over a decade ago we stumbled, or were pushed, into a way of investing our meager savings in undeveloped land in, of all places, New York State—within sight of the Empire State Building!

This book tells the story, instructively and amusingly we hope, of how Dame Fortune, abetted by good friends, had to practically knock us over the heads and rub our noses in opportunity before we saw it.

It tells also how, after having been made aware of our opportunity, we went on to achieve a substantial degree of security by making modest investments in unimproved land.

"Why land?" We'll answer that question in Chapter Three. But a good clue to the answer may be found in a statement made not long ago by J. Fred Talley, real estate commissioner for the state of Arizona.

"We are at present," said Commissioner Talley, "in the midst of one of the three great migrations in recorded history. First, there was the migration of the Children of Israel through the Red Sea. Then the great migration during the latter part of the last century when our immigration laws permitted the great shifts of population from Europe to America.

"These two are being dwarfed today by the staggering number of people who are finally taking Horace Greeley's advice, 'Go West, young man, go West!'"

This staggering mass migration is a matter of great concern to men like Commissioner Talley, Commissioner Gordon of California, Commissioner Jensen of Oregon, and the commissioners of other affected states. The problem is complex and it is not the same in each area. For instance in California, where the large areas of cheap land needed for the questionable raw land subdivisions are almost nonexistent now, the problem is not so much that of the unethical promoter selling California land as the problem of the promoter selling the questionable land of other states to Californians.

In states where there is still much third-class acreage in remote regions that can be scuffed up into parcels by a grader or a bulldozer, the problem is compounded. For then the commissioners must not only protect the citizens of their own states against being swindled by misrepresentation but they must also try to protect the unwary mail-order buyer in other states who, having been swindled, may be inclined to misjudge *all* land in the seller's state. To further complicate the matter and confound the officials who must try to frame effective laws for every contingency, there is the promoter who lives in one state, sells land by mail and other forms of advertising in a *second* state to citizens of a *third* state. Understandably, it is enough to make responsible real estate commissioners a bit short tempered. And some of them are.

How widespread are the abuses? What effect have they had on western land as an investment? How effective are present laws? Will federal intervention be necessary and will it cure the evils? Is there any good raw land left? These are a few of the questions we wanted answered because of our own western land-investment program. So we took to the road to find out.

After talking with real estate commissioners, governors,

development organizations, Better Business bureaus, chambers of commerce, newspaper editors, land wholesalers, ranchers, promoters, subdividers, city planners, and just plain citizens who had bought western land, we reached some personal over-all conclusions as to the correct answers. They may be stated simply as follows:

First—apparently only a small percentage of the land promoters in the western states deserve to be severely disciplined for questionable or dishonest practices.

Second—the great majority of developers are ethical businessmen and are an integral, even vital, part of the machinery of America's orderly expansion. As such they are in grave danger of being unjustly judged by the public because of the widely publicized activities of the unscrupulous few.

Third—we found a great need for a book that would state the situation simply, in layman's language—a book that could be used by the average small investor to reduce his chances of being "taken" by a land shark by telling how they operate so he may recognize their alluring come-on's—a book that will further protect him by showing him *what makes land valuable* and *where* such land is likely to be found.

We sincerely hope that THE SIMPLE TRUTH ABOUT WESTERN LAND INVESTMENT is such a book.

Postscript: Since the foregoing introduction was written we have traveled several thousands of miles reviewing areas. The results of this trip will be found in this *revised edition* together with new photographic evidence of the changing trend in land development all across the country.

Leland Frederick Cooley
Lee Morrison Cooley
Incline Village, Nevada,
September 1967.

THE SIMPLE TRUTH
ABOUT WESTERN
LAND INVESTMENT

THE SOLID GOLD GUN
AT OUR HEADS!

Since the first man with the first club defended a patch of
ground within a reasonable radius of the mouth of his cave,
the possession of land has been the prime factor in acquiring
real wealth and security.

Over the years we have been given many books on real
estate and we've read the advertisements of subdividers who
quote everybody from Aesop to Bernard Baruch on the subject of land being the only true and sure foundation for a
great fortune.

Frankly we are not surprised that all these men of great
wisdom understood that. It's such an obvious fact. In fact we
feel pretty stupid for having seen this truth right before us for
years and having waited until we were middle-aged to act. It
would have been far easier to act even two decades ago. It is
not fiction that our present holdings would have been worth
many thousands of dollars more.

Back in the days when there was a lot of good, unused land in every state and still more public land in territories—enough to make thirty or more new states in time—it wasn't too hard to find a good piece of inexpensive land. If a man wanted urban land he bought low-cost acreage on the fringe of an established community and before too long he found his property was "in town." As the town grew to a city the land often wound up being "downtown." Cut up into city lots its value often increased a thousandfold in his own lifetime.

Later on in this book we are going to trace the growth patterns of our great cities. They are so great now we've had to apply a new name to them. They are now being called megalopolises. What a remarkable people, the Greeks! They truly *do* have a word for it. To properly label these sprawling new communities they gave us the word *megalo* adapted from *megas* meaning "great or giant in size" and the word *polis* meaning "city." Within the next few decades a mere metropolis or "chief city" will be nothing but a major district of the megalopolis of which it is a part. We're not very Greek but we have a word for them too: We call them, "*Megalocto-puses.*"

The forces which are causing these great conglomerate communities to reach out, and the *directions* in which they are certain to grow, are the two magic keys to future fortunes in real estate.

Stripped to the bare bones, the *purpose* of this book is to explain those forces in everyday language, to predict the directions in which their main pressures will be exerted, and to do so in a manner that will enable any average small investor to go out and find relatively inexpensive bulk or "raw" land which, within a few short years, may become the basis for a sizable fortune.

As we said in the introduction, we know the method works: We have made it work for us. And it has worked for several of our good friends. We hope to show you how to make it work too. But before we do we'd like to say two things: First, we are *NOT* in the land business so we have no ax to grind . . . nothing to sell; and second, despite the fact that our method is simple—just plain common sense—*no* method of making sound real estate investment will work *unless you make it work*. You don't have to do it alone—in fact we think it is foolish to try to—for the same reason that it would be foolish for you to try to teach yourself to fly an airplane. Everybody needs help until he learns. We did too. But we believe that THE SIMPLE TRUTH ABOUT WESTERN LAND IN-VESTMENT can speed up the learning process. By using the principles outlined in this book—*and by enlisting the serv-ices of a reputable realtor*—you can make it happen a lot sooner for yourselves than it did for us. We had some tough lessons to learn. This book is an attempt to spare you the pain of learning the hard way and to show you how an average couple with an average income can go out, today, and make reasonable land purchases which, within ten years or so, may be the foundation for a real fortune. We've repeated that on purpose.

The formula is so simple that it could be stated in five pages. But we feel, to fully understand it, we should take a little longer and spell it out in terms of our own experiences and the experiences of others whom we know.

Although this book deals primarily with western land be-cause the investment spotlight is on our part of the country now (and the *investigation* spotlight too, thank goodness!) the principle applies equally anywhere in the world where population is increasing and available land is decreasing.

When we're trying to get an idea through our heads we find it more interesting, and enlightening, too, to have it ex-plained in terms of true stories, dramatic examples that illus-trate a basic idea. Charts and pictures help of course, and we'll use some where they do help. But telling the actual stories of how someone followed the plan or formula or system, made it work, and made money in land, is the most convincing illustration.

If we tell you how it began with us, we think you'll see the fundamental principle clearly right from Chapter One and it won't be necessary for some friend to hold a gun to your head and force you to march to your good fortune, as was the case with us!

The year was 1954. The place was our apartment in Manhattan. The New York Boat Show was still running at Grand Central Palace on Lexington Avenue. (A dairy farm was said to have occupied the area a hundred years earlier. The Income Tax Bureau occupies it now!)

Captain Ken Stein and his wife, Eunice, who operate the ferry service from Sayville, Long Island, to several Fire Island resort towns, called rather late and asked if they could come up.

We put on the coffeepot, dusted off the end tables, and waited to greet them. Almost without ceremony Captain Ken said, "Look, you two—you're going to buy some land!"

For one reason or another, reasons familiar to most married couples, land was about the last thing on earth we figured to be buying. New tires, maybe, or an auxiliary tank for the old outboard, but land? Out of the question! That's for rich folks! When we didn't react, Captain Stein repeated, "I said, you're going to buy some land! And if you argue about it, *we're* going to buy it for you—in your name—and hold it until you can pay for it!"

After half an hour of stubborn resistance we agreed to drive out to Sayville when it warmed up a bit and look over this throbbing bargain that would put us in hock for the rest of our unnatural lives.

January went by and February and March came tagging along as usual. We shivered and cussed through March and paid rapt attention to ground hogs, crocuses, and the *Farmers' Almanac*. April finally arrived.

For a time we breathed easily because we thought Captain Ken and Eunice had forgotten their threat, or their promise, or whatever it was. But early in April the phone rang.

"The ice is out of the bay now," Ken said cheerfully. "Drive on up this Sunday and we'll fire up one of the ferries and run across to the Island. They'll be starting to work on the subdivision soon. I want you to see it at its worst before you buy!"

We did! Everything was at its worst that Sunday . . . the weather, the boat, Great South Bay, our dispositions. We were hardly in a buying frame of mind.

Huddled against a freezing rain—"flying sherbet" Captain Ken called it—we braced ourselves in the pilothouse of a narrow-beamed, former rumrunner refitted and rechristened *Fire Island Pines Number Two*. Expertly handled, she sliced, or rather sluiced her way through the troughs of waves stacked three feet high by a sudden "easter".

It took thirty minutes to cross four and seven tenths miles of water. When we finally picked up the navigational aids, (long stakes stuck in the mud flats by the oystermen), and ran into the shelter of the "harbor," we were both in a frame of mind not only not to buy but to send the Steins the doctor bills certain to result.

After much maneuvering Ken brought the big ferry alongside a partially finished length of bulkheading in a large dredged-out cranberry bog. He asked us to visualize it as a $200,000 yacht harbor. A few minutes later we were picking our way down an incompleted section of boardwalk which we were told would be one of the "main thoroughfares" of a subdivision being called Fire Island Pines by its imaginative promoter, Dr. Warren Smadbeck.

Numbed to the bone, we stumbled and pushed our way through virgin stands of holly, poison ivy, poison sumac, scrub oak, and the strange flat-topped pines that are found nowhere else but along the sandspit that forms the incredible offshore barrier reef called Fire Island.

Following survey stakes we came to a particularly fine stand of pines. A doe about ready to drop a fawn moved away without too much concern. A short distance beyond a red fox ran along the hollow-ground blade of a long sand dune. All around us the wild blueberries were beginning to put out buds; brambles of raspberries lay tangled and matted like the abandoned, barbed-wire, outer defenses of some long-forgotten stronghold.

"This is where we've bought *our* lots," enthused Ken, "and we think you should take these two lots next to us. It's the prettiest part of the island!"

When we continued to gape in mute disbelief at the un-improved patches of sand which Ken had somehow identified as lots 125 and 126, Eunice smiled sympathetically and murmured, "It does sort of take your breath away, doesn't it?"

We looked at each other with that special perception given to husbands and wives who have suffered much together. "The whole prospect leaves us speechless," we agreed.

Seizing our limp arms, the Steins maneuvered us into position for the kill. We slogged southward through ankle-deep sand until we topped the dune that stretched like a great, frozen fluid barrier against the battering Atlantic. The force of the icy wind stunned us and the rolling thunder of the surf deafened us. Speechless we were, but, thank heavens, not sightless. Stretched away for a dozen miles to the east and a like distance to the west was one of the most beautiful white sand beaches we'd seen anywhere in the world. And, as though Mother Nature herself had decided to join the conspiracy, there was a sudden lifting and rending of the dark cloud cover and shafts of warm sun drove through to us. At the same moment, off to the west, there was a bright point of glare like the sun striking a distant mirror.

Captain Ken saw it and smiled. "Empire State Building," he announced. "It's only forty-six air miles away." He probed his pipe bowl with a finger that must have been made of asbestos, and added, "In a couple of years, when they finish Southern State Parkway, it'll only take an hour and a half, tops, to drive to Sayville from Manhattan."

Seven days (and sleepless nights) later the Steins cranked up the ferry for the second preseason trip to meet Sales Manager Edward Olson at Fire Island Pines. It took an hour for us to buy lots 125 and 126.

From April until June we alternately blessed our friends and cursed them and ourselves. But when the summer arrived and we returned to find crews carrying out orders ahead of schedule, we sought out the Steins and humbly confessed our earlier misgivings, asked their forgiveness, and urged them to predict which side of the harbor, east or west, would grow into "the" part of town.

We agreed with their predictions. By the end of summer we had borrowed enough to purchase several more lots and had signed a contract for the lovely beach home that we were to name Casa del Sol, House of the Sun.

What happened at Fire Island Pines was entirely predictable. Dr. Smadbeck had foreseen it; Captain Stein had foreseen it, and, thank Heavens, in the end we were made to see it too. We urged a number of our friends to buy. Like us, they have all made money by holding on; and for an extra tax-free dividend we all have had one of the most beautiful beaches on earth on which to summer. Not too long back *Holiday* magazine chose the ten most beautiful beaches in the world. The glistening white ribbon of sand that lies right below our summer house was one of them.

Eight years ago some of those lots were still being purchased for as little as $750. Today the least of them will bring seven times that. Recently we refused a 1000 per cent profit on two of our remaining lots. Taxes have increased, to be sure (a good index of growth, if a painful one!), but not nearly so quickly as the value of the property. Net profit taken today would be real and impressive . . . and as anti-inflationary as profit in dollars can be these days.

Actually the wonderful adventures we had establishing the town of Fire Island Pines (it was a conservative family community then, not the ultra-sophisticated resort it has since become) would make an adventure book in itself.

Skeptics called it a "land promotion" or a "get-rich-quick subdivision." Well, it *was* both of those. It was a land promotion because new places do not get started without imaginative promoters to spark them. (Not all promoters or land developers follow through as thoroughly as Dr. Smadbeck and his crew did at "The Pines.") It *was* a "get-rich-quick subdivision" alright too . . . and those of us who bought early and held on and followed the plan laid down in the Property Owners' Association by-laws did "get-rich-quick" in the sense that our original investments multiplied many times in actual worth and enriched our lives in other nontaxable ways that have given us golden memories to cherish for years to come. And we still hold some of the original purchases!

For the Cooleys, that was the start . . . just about ten years ago. Since then we have applied the simple, the obvious lessons learned at The Pines (we can still see the Empire State Building on a clear day) to a number of other places. Captain Fred Stein, Jr., brother of Captain Ken, called us in the mid-1950s and asked us to visit at his Florida home on the beautiful St. Lucie River at Rio, across the bay from the thriving city of Stuart.

We accepted and were driven up from the Palm Beach airport in less than an hour. A week later, after subscribing to the local newspaper (a must in possible investment areas) we returned to New York City convinced that this was the "coming place" on Florida's fabulous east coast. A short time later we purchased seven acres of beautiful flat land right across the highway from the Stein's new Casa Marina boat landing and just a short distance from Frances Langford's beautiful resort, Langford Hall. The land was not yet on the market, being part of an estate. Fred Stein had heard about it, we knew the land, so we engaged a local attorney (another must to our way of thinking) and arranged the purchase through the heirs.

We've had several offers to sell this land for a nice profit. We have refused. Why? Because the census and later research shows that the Stuart–Jensen Beach–Rio area is just beginning its real growth. We knew that great growth would come to our area sooner or later. How? We looked at Florida's past to predict its future. The trends were all written there. We read all of the old news magazines and back issues of the *Stuart News* that we could find. When they know you are interested, alert real estate men and women help too. One of them sent us a copy of a *Kiplinger Letter* which reported some interesting facts and made even more interesting projections. We decided to hold. We're still holding—and we'll continue to because with Florida one of the fastest growing states in the Union, with an all-year climate, with some of the greatest recreational land in the world lying along its full length, the growing population, or *people pressure* as we call it, is already making Stuart's growth phenomenal. We have learned that some prescience and a lot of patience are basic ingredients for successful land investment too. But nothing substitutes for factual knowledge of a general area. So far as the Stuart area was concerned we got a lot of factual knowledge firsthand from the Steins, from the local realtors, and from the *Stuart News*.

In Fred Stein's comfortable lapstrake skiff we went out to the Gulf Stream sailfishing. We got "outside" through St. Lucie Inlet. It's not the safest inlet in the world at the moment, but is only a matter of time before people pressure will get it stabilized. When that is done the Stuart–Jensen Beach–

Rio area will have more than earned its rightful title as "the sailfishing capital of the world."

And did we get fish! Every size and shape from grunt to marlin. One day we explored the Indian River, part of the famous Inland Waterway that offers safe passage for small boats all the way from New Jersey to Miami. On another day we went up the North Fork of the St. Lucie River and fished for large-mouthed bass and snook. On still another day we chose the South Fork, sailed to its head, and entered the canal. Negotiating the locks we soon came to the remarkable Lake Okeechobee. Had we wanted to, we could have proceeded by boat across the state of Florida to Fort Meyers on the Gulf of Mexico. We know of no other area in the United States that offers more variety of travel, of fishing and hunting, of absolutely wonderful outdoor living—and for virtually twelve months out of the year.

Does it take a giant intellect to reason that if hundreds of others had discovered the area, had come to stay or come to vacation as we had, that literally thousands of others would do the same in the coming years? We discovered the Stuart–Rio area five years ago. Since then the population of the entire area has exploded with new developments. The Stuart census doubled from 1950 to 1960. Florida topped the *growth* list on the census at 76.6 per cent. Indications are that it will more than double in the next decade. People pressure again. And since we continue to make *more people* but cannot make *more land,* people pressure must drive land prices upward as demand increases for living and recreational room. 'Twas ever thus—but never so much as now.

In 1958, when business brought us back home to Southern California, we found ourselves in the midst of still another fabulous people pressure area.

Coming into California at the rate of more than 580,000 persons per year, the coastal plain was burgeoning. Places where we had hunted jack rabbits on old Spanish rangeland had become towns and cities in the intervening years. Seeing them there before us, our credulity was still taxed.

With profits taken from Fire Island property purchased but a few years earlier, we began consciously applying the simple common-sense formula that had taken us so long to evolve.

But western land is another story—or so we thought—because there seemed to be so much more of it. Each weekend we drove many miles. For the first year we did nothing but look. The money from eastern land was drawing generous interest in two banks and a savings and loan institution in Laguna Beach. Those impressive bank buildings, by the way, are located approximately where Mother and Dad Cooley spent their honeymoon camping on the deserted beach in 1904 after a three-day horse and wagon trip through rolling hills from Riverside via historic Laguna Canyon. We make the same trip today in one hour on brand-new freeways through solidly settled communities. We are never out of sight of a gas station. Not very good for the scenery perhaps but very, very good for land values!

Just about thirteen months after returning from a twenty-one year stay in New York City, we made our first raw land purchase in the Golden West.

We bought in the Emerald Triangle section of the booming Antelope Valley, just about the same number of miles from the Los Angeles City Hall as Fire Island Pines is from the Empire State Building.

Very shortly now we will tell you why we chose the Antelope Valley for our *major* raw land investment and you will begin to see clearly, by actual demonstration, how to apply the simple common-sense formula to the selection of your own inexpensive investment land.

Before we get down to "brass tacks" let us say once again that this book deals primarily with the finding and purchasing of so called "raw" western land.

In our own investment plan for the future we may buy improved property such as lots and plots closer in, if they seem to be exceptional buys. But by far the greater part of our investment money will be spent on acreage "in the path of progress," acreage susceptible of large price increases with a minimum outlay of taxes and improvement money because of people pressure in the general area.

More sophisticated investors may laugh at us. Let them. We are writers, not land operators or, for that matter, professional land investors. Land is not our business, it is our hobby . . . and a highly profitable and enjoyable one too. The searching for it is more than half the fun . . . and the wonderful people we meet in the process and the local history we discover is a huge, nontaxable profit that can never be taken away. The search for a few simple facts has become an adventure that has taken us into six western states, into governors' mansions, state houses, chambers of commerce, development boards, Better Business bureaus, state museums and libraries, all in a quest for knowledge that never fails to be an absorbing adventure as well.

We're not suggesting that all of you who read this carry the search as far as we do. But you can if you want to. And when you finally buy, you'll buy with confidence and you'll experience the deep pleasure that comes from being convinced that you've made the correct buy for you.

When you buy it may be from a subdivider. The men of this profession are sometimes justly criticized; more often they are unjustly criticized. Let's see how they fit into the picture.

2

A FEW KIND WORDS ABOUT SUBDIVIDERS IN GENERAL AND LAND IN PARTICULAR

In general, subdividers are a much maligned group. They don't really deserve to be. But, as always in our society, a lot of honest men in any profession can be tarred by a brush carelessly slung by a few unethical promoters who would be bad operators no matter what endeavor they chose.

Mining deals, oil deals, and land deals have always been "the unholy three" as far as crooked operators are concerned. The reason is simple; over the years quick fortunes have been made by speculating in them. And who among us can honestly say that he would have gumption enough to deafen his ears to a convincing pitch that sounded like a "sure thing"?

Texas Guinan was right when she greeted every customer to her famous speakeasy with a hearty, "Hello sucker!" because Barnum was right when he said, "There's a sucker born every minute." We're all suckers for something. It's usually a "something" that promises sudden riches. You cannot legislate larceny from the hearts of men. The ultimate answer lies in education, not regulation. But education on such a scale is a long, slow process. In spite of concerted efforts to suppress the gambling instinct, we all like to take a chance. Human nature hasn't changed and it's not likely to. So long as we remain hopeful, acquisitive mortals, most of us are going to fall for one swindle or another. Unethical land dividers know this—and they trade on it with misleading promises, false advertising, and downright lies. Those who trade on the desire of our senior citizens for a secure little place of their own, free and clear, are the most vicious of all.

Not long ago the problem had become so urgent in our Western states—and in some of the Eastern states also—that concerned state officials began revamping their real estate subdivision laws to prevent unscrupulous "Paradise Peddlers" from bilking thousands of buyers of millions of dollars through the sale of desert land, often located so far off the beaten path as to be virtually uninhabitable.* There are some sticky legal issues at stake having to do with the jurisdictional control of interstate sales and advertising. There are fundamental issues involved, too, such as continuing encroachment by the federal government into the rights of the sovereign states. The issue reaches as far as the Constitution. Insofar as is practical, the states want to do the police job themselves. The problem is complex, but don't be alarmed; you don't have to become a *land lawyer* to protect yourself when you purchase *if* you enlist the services of an ethical, licensed expert in land. That person would be any reputable real estate broker or realtor. We'll explain the difference between the two later. You may not know it. We didn't for some years.

Despite the terrific clamor being set up by the press and magazines about crooked land promotions, the great majority of developments are conceived and executed by pro-

* See authors' statement to Senate Banking and Currency Sub-Committee, August 12, 1966, re Senate Bill S 2672.

moters who operate well within the boundaries of accepted practice.

Before joining our voices in the chorus of criticism directed at them for coloring their advertising with flagrant exaggeration, let's just remember that they are not the sole offenders on this score. Just take a look at almost any ad.

This tendency to exaggerate in order to sell is a national ailment brought on by the need to outdo the competition. It is accepted tacitly as a "necessary evil" in our system and, whether we like it or not, it is also one of the prime movers of our economy. The "hard sell" has been directly responsible for much of what we call our progress.

Right or wrong, the hard sell technique is with us . . . and it would seem to be no less honest when used to sell real estate than when used to sell any other commodity. The problem is both economic and moral. And it may be that the day is coming when state and federal restraints will have to be applied more generally in *all* selling simply to protect us from ourselves. After all, isn't that what a speed limit does? If we all exercised the common sense God is supposed to have given us, such signs would not be necessary; we would need no laws to protect our most precious possessions, our lives. No, there seems to be a built-in "bilk factor" in all of us. If this were not true our derisive laughter long since would have silenced the exaggerators and rid the press and air of extravagant claims that should insult our intelligence. The trouble is that our intelligence is *not* being insulted because the message never gets to it. Instead, it is happily absorbed by that nonthinking, automatically reacting part of us called our emotional selves. We don't reason, we react. And we may be sure that those who want to sell us something have made intensive studies of our reactions. Each day they are learning more about which buttons to press in order to induce in us a desire to do or to have something. The large advertising agencies have departments full of professional psychologists who do nothing but explore motivational appeals that can make us want to buy their clients' products. And one of the easiest desires to stimulate in the average man is the desire to buy a plot of ground that he can call his own.

Strangely enough very few buyers of land ever get truly skinned in the long run. Some buyers find they have to sell at a loss for reasons beyond their control, but in this country there is hardly an owner of a house and lot or a patch of acreage who, if he has held it for five years or more, could not dispose of it for a good net profit. With sales resistance almost zero where a "dream ranch" is concerned, the land dividers feel that they must outdo each other to attract our dollars . . . and that is particularly true if their "paradise" happens to be in the most remote reaches of the typical desert region we call "West Hellangone." Conveniently located in the heart of nowhere, they must make their acre-and-a-quarter or two-and-a-half-acre parcels sound like they are within easy walking distance of both oceans and on the very shores of America's most fabulous inland-water wonderland.

In Arizona they told us the story (perhaps not apocryphal), of the eager land divider who saw the same mirage three days hand running. He promptly bought the land between him and it and subdivided it into waterfront lots.

To us this tall tale is not half so symptomatic of a widespread desire to defraud as it is indicative of the overwhelming desire of the average man to own his piece of the U.S.A. We think he should. There's no better investment on earth, no pun intended.

In the last chapter we are going to introduce you to several enterprising land developers. Professional land men are a colorful lot, in many respects not unlike the visionary pioneers who preceded them. Some of them are controversial. All of them are men who must surmount huge obstacles to get things accomplished. The best of them are indispensable to orderly suburban growth under America's system of free enterprise.

If you who are reading this are anything at all like us then you, too, have heard dozens of stories, many firsthand, of friends and friends of friends who have made good investments in land . . . not only western land but in good land everywhere in the country.

Not long ago we appeared at the Los Angeles Ebell Club's Book Section luncheon to speak on the state of the modern novel. After the speeches were over a woman came up to us and said, "I enjoyed the talks so much, but I particularly enjoyed the true stories you told about land." We like true stories about land. They illustrate what we want to say better than all the charts and graphs in the libraries.

A few years before he died, the famous actor Leo Carrillo was talking about California land. We told him the sad story of some members of our family who sold out the remnants of our own Spanish Grant, El Rancho de las Flores, about ten years ago. They received two hundred dollars an acre, including a good farmhouse.

Leo sighed, "Where land is concerned, amigos, I don't think wisdom comes with age. Sometimes I think the older ones take land for granted. Thank God my people have always known its value. And they taught it to me."

Indeed they must have! Leo Carrillo (pronounced, by the way, Cah-*reel*-yo) never seemed content unless he owned land. He had a beautiful place back of Santa Monica and nearly five thousand acres not far north of El Camino Real near the town of Carlsbad, between Los Angeles and San Diego. Leo said he paid less than $50 an acre for that land back in the Thirties. We have been told that he had retained most of it in his estate. A realtor in the area said the land today is worth, conservatively, from three to five thousand dollars an acre . . . an increase of 6000 per cent in thirty years! What caused it? Two things, people pressure and ample water. Remember those two ingredients; *the simple truth, in fact the whole truth about western land value, is founded upon them.*

You might say, "Well, if we earned several thousand dollars a week back in the days of easy income tax we could have done that too!" That's right, you could have. But we know average, small land investors who have done as well, relatively.

Let's take the example of two friends of ours, Milton and Penny Katz. Penny is a native daughter of California and a believer in land. Milton is a New Yorker who fell in love with Penny and California simultaneously—two loves that have never wavered. True to the tradition of our native daughters, Penny insisted that they buy some acreage when Milton came to settle in the San Fernando Valley. That was in 1944.

Fitting the price to the purse they went out to the town of Van Nuys and purchased ten acres of an old walnut orchard. The price was $9000, or $900 an acre.

The next year, in order to help finance the new home they had planned, they sold off 2½ acres for $3500. The following year they sold off another 2½-acre parcel, this time for $4000. Their house stood on one of the two remaining 2½-acre parcels.

One of those they subdivided into ten city lots. Six of those lots sold immediately for $2500 each. They held the remaining four lots for several years. People pressure in Van Nuys sent the price up to $5500 per lot. They sold the four lots for $22,000 and still kept their beautiful home on 2½ acres of prime land. Three quarters of their original land purchase had returned them a gross profit of $20,500.

Recently they sold the house and grounds for $55,000 in order to make another business purchase. Milt is satisfied that he did the best thing as he saw it at the time. "But," he says, "too much hindsight can make you unhappy too. If I were to do it all over again I'd have subdivided the ten acres into forty city lots. If I had done so those lots would have brought $8000 each by now. That would have meant a gross profit of $311,000 on a $9000 original investment!"

Of course Milt knew that taxes and subdivision costs would have brought that down considerably. But even so the net capital gain would have been well over $200,000.

These figures are not fiction. Profits in land have been taken by hundreds of average people in the west—thousands perhaps—people who were lucky enough or perspicacious enough to buy *in the path of progress.* In the real estate investment business people pressure can turn pennies into handsome pensions. The reason it doesn't happen more often is simple—*most people don't hold long enough.*

Sometimes long enough isn't very long.

This is not a Southern California phenomenon. The same story can be duplicated hundreds of times in the San Francisco area, in Portland, in Seattle, in Spokane, in Phoenix, in Tucson, in Reno and Las Vegas, in all the great cities and surrounding areas in every state in the Union. The reason is always the same—*people pressure. We keep making more people but we cannot make more land.*

Sometimes people pressure operates more slowly. We have a writer friend in Connecticut who came originally from a farm in Ohio. We asked if we could repeat the story he told us recently. He said, "Yes, but use my initials, will you? We are in negotiation on that Ohio land now. We think we might sell this time." So we'll call him R.B. and quote part of his own true story:

Sixty-odd years ago that part of Ohio wasn't exactly primitive but it certainly was pastoral. People lived and died and were never more than thirty miles from home. Many had never been as distant as Cincinnati. All they knew about the city was the general direction. It was very understandable—there was little means of getting there. The roads, three inches deep in lime dust in the summer (from the limestone beds), were six inches deep in lime soup in the wet weather. Three miles away from the 100-acre farm was a branch of the Pennsylvania Railroad. Three miles in the other direction was a spur of the Norfolk & Western. That was the transportation.

Farmers used to haul hay and vegetables for extra cash, and so had a glimpse of the great city. They'd return home with city clothing and bolts of dress goods for their wives as though they were Marco Polos.

All of this was changed with the growth of the interurban electric traction lines. We had one in our neighborhood. It was strictly a stock sales promotion deal, but it did open up the farm country and served a strip of land about eight miles on each side of its single track. It had both freight and passenger service—though calves and hogs rode almost as well as the farmers. Land that had been worth forty to fifty dollars an acre became worth eighty to one hundred.[1]

We had our first offer of $100 per acre as soon as the traction line was built. Land values were stabilized at that level until World War I. After the war came the beginning of the better-roads movement. A blacktop job, built in 1922, hoisted our land to $150 an acre. It climbed to $175 per acre until the 1929 depression and then there were no sales at any figure.

Land values climbed very slowly until the Second World War. New industries brought in new people. Soon they were offering $500 for enough land for a house, a victory garden and a garage. My mother spurned them all. But

[1] R.B.'s mother purchased the 100 acres plus houses and equipment for $5500 in 1900.

due to public utility pressure she had to sell enough land for one electric tower. The initial offer was one thousand dollars. She held out and got $7500.

After the war, real estate developers started making offers for the land—trick deals of all sorts, down payments and second mortgages. They all got the grand turn down. Meanwhile smaller parcels of land around us were built up into garden apartments, small shopping centers, small country places. A three-acre plot brought from $3500 to $5000.

The last offer my mother had was $100,000 for the hundred acres for which she had paid $5500. No deal!

Since that time a new federal road has been proposed along our property. A syndicate came along with a deal—$11,000 per acre for a shopping center and $10,000 per acre for garden apartments.

And there the deal rests. We are in no hurry. . . .

If you have been following R.B.'s arithmetic, you can see that allowing ten acres for a shopping center (very conservative) and ninety acres for garden apartments, he and his family would stand to receive well over a million dollars for the 100 acres. That is Ohio. The principle is the same in *any* area. There was a time, well within the memory of persons alive today, when that part of Ohio might well have been called "West Hellangone" too!

Because this book is intended to do two useful things, inform and instruct, we may find ourselves saying the same thing in several different ways in order to emphasize the importance of basic truths about one of the finest investments left on this overcrowded earth—western land.

The three important things to remember in the story of R.B.'s Ohio farm (which can now make him a bona fide millionaire) are these:

- *The family held the land;*
- *The electric interurban traction company opened up the area to cheap transportation.*
- *The first blacktop road came through to supplement the traction line.*

Because R.B.'s mother insisted upon holding, the other two factors, interurban trains and good roads, increased the value of her 100 acres.

The one underlying factor, of course, was people pressure.

The operation of these factors and their result can be expressed in elementary mathematics like this:

TIME + PEOPLE PRESSURE + WATER + TRANSPORTATION = INCREASED LAND VALUE.

In Chapter Seven we are going to show you in detail how people pressure develops and how to predict the directions it will take. Once you know that, you have the key to the simple truth about good land investments, not only in the west but everywhere. As we said before, we are writing primarily about western land in this book because the focus of national attention is on the current western land boom. But the principle applies to *any* land *anywhere*.

3

WHY INVEST IN THE WEST?

It's time now to pose a question that some of you may have on your minds. The essence of the question is, "Why invest in western land—or *any land* for that matter—when I could put my money in stocks and bonds or perhaps in improved real estate?"

The answer is simple: *Don't* put all of your investment eggs in any *one* basket.

We have done very well with stocks and bonds. And once we were tempted to buy into an expensive cooperative apartment in New York City. By consulting hindsight we know now that if we had we would have shown a respectable gross profit and a fair net profit—and we would have had our living too. But we were afraid of such problems as management by committee, continual battles to maintain city, state, and federal tax legislation favorable to such cooperative ownership, rising service and maintenance costs, and a few other difficulties that did not seem to exist in the purchase of raw or semideveloped land.

It is true that, in order to maintain the progress we wanted at Fire Island Pines in Suffolk County, New York, we had to become the first president and secretary respectively of the Property Owners' Association. That was a lot of hard work. But it was also a wonderful experience because we all learned together—we and our board of directors—about the complex problems that beset a growing community. In time teamwork built the town. But no more such projects for us! We leave that enlightening adventure to younger couples.

We said we've done well with stocks and bonds. We have. But we've had some nervous moments too. Every time the market gets shaky so do the investors. We've seen the current market value of some of our "blue chips" decrease as much as 50 per cent in a few hours. We've never seen a piece of land do that, not even land adjacent to an area where a nationally publicized tragedy took place. True, the market for the land in that neighborhood slowed down for a few months because a huge recreational development was aborted. But values are stable again now. Recently the president of the realty board serving that area told us that basic land values have increased substantially since then. Grandfather Cooley spoke the truth when he said, "A lot of poor souls have killed themselves on their land but none of them ever hurt the land much."

We've taken some nice capital gains profits out of good stocks. Whenever our stockbroker calls we listen because, like the realtor, he, too, is a qualified expert in his field with vast research facilities at his disposal. Information, *accurate information*, is the secret of judging any investment and many men are rich today because they have learned how to accumulate it.

Perhaps we just have a better "feel" for land. But there's another thing too; we show a net profit on our ten-year-hold land that far exceeds the profits taken from the stocks we've held for the same length of time. Here's an example:

In 1954 we bought fifty shares of stock in a leading oil company, a "blue chip" stock it is called. We paid 51½ per share, or $2575 plus the broker's commission. At about the same time we also purchased two lots in Suffolk County, New York, for $1200 each or a total of $2400. The seller paid the commission.

Eight years later, in 1962, the stock was worth only $45 a share if we had wanted to sell it. It had earned $1098 in dividends, upon which we had paid income tax. We sold the two lots in that same year. Their actual market value had risen to $6000 each. The sale grossed us $12,000. After deducting the taxes paid during those years, the broker's commission, and the original investment, we had a net profit of $8180 upon which we were able to take a favorable capital gain.

As of now, ten years later, the oil stock is about the same as when we paid for it. In short, there has been no capital gain possible on that investment during these years.

This is not an isolated example. We can show you similar figures on a piece of improved property—a beach house—where annual leases returned a wonderful profit when reckoned against depreciation. In the end, when we sold the improved property, the net profit to us was 300 per cent, *not counting* the five years of rent free "dividend living" we'd had. The lot under that particular house increased in value from $1200 to $6000 during that same time. Many stocks have made spectacular increases in value. However, very few stocks return more than a safe and consistent 4 per cent net over the years. And if the market price of the stock increases substantially, the interest return can diminish rapidly unless the increase is based on actual book value increases and not transitory market demand. But too often the price-to-earnings ratio is unrealistic. In order to keep the dividend interest ratio the same, the earnings paid out in dividends must increase too.

A good example in our own portfolio is a major picture studio's stock. We bought modest amounts several years ago at 59. At this writing it is down to 30. In this instance we were advised to continue to purchase as it declined in order to "average down" and increase our chances of "getting out even."

Generally that is not good investment practice. But after seeing some of the marvelous pictures in production now, we are confident the stock will come back up again. We are holding. But the point to watch is the percentage yield as an investment. When the recent dividend payment remained the same as it had been when the stock was at the higher price, a friend called up and said encouragingly, "Look at that, folks! With the stock at 30 you're making a solid 5 per cent!" (The dividend has since come down.) Not exactly true. We *didn't buy* the stock at 30. We bought at 59, and continued to buy as it went down. The *average* cost of our stock is around 38½. The average return is actually considerably less than 5 per cent. Figures don't lie—but well-intentioned friends *figure!*

Speaking of being well-intentioned; it is not our intention to unfavorably compare stocks with land. There are stocks and stocks; and there is land and land. The great choice of, and the complexities of, the investments available in both fields make even an exhaustive comparison futile. Generally speaking there are fine investment opportunities in both areas. But, still speaking generally, for us—an average, modestly moneyed pair of investors who have neither the skill nor the desire to study the stock market as persistently and profoundly as is necessary to equate its complicated data —we feel safer investing in raw and semideveloped land. The factors affecting its value move more slowly; the long range trend is uniformly up, as indeed it has been in the stock market; but in raw and semideveloped land the averages don't fluctuate so much so quickly. Nothing is as "nervous-making" to us as watching the daily fluctuation of the stock market!

There have been booms and busts in land too—a lot of them. But we can truthfully say that we've never seen a piece of speculative land lose *all* of its value and cease to exist. The same may not be said for several speculative stocks we've been touted onto in the past decade. The companies have simply ceased to exist. As one old-timer said to us, "Well, you folks just remember this; if you buy land and they blow it up, you still own the hole in the ground!"

There is another advantage to raw acreage or semideveloped land as we see it; while no investment for which you spend dollars is *inflationproof*, well-chosen land offers some built-in compensations that many other types of investments don't seem to have. For instance, good land well located in people pressure areas often will rise in value so quickly that the increase in value will outstrip the decrease in purchasing power of the dollar.

This will be an oversimplification for the professional finance man, but this book isn't written for him. The point is, *the principle is correct*. In such a situation you will probably get so much more for your land when you sell it that in a sense the actual gain you will have made will be greater than that possible in most other opportunities open to the small investor.

To use just one comparison, if you had paid into an annuity until it reached maturity and you wished to cash it out, you would be paid (in these times) in *inflated* or *depreciated* dollars. Although you would receive the full amount of the matured face value of the policy, the dollars you paid in were worth more than the dollars you would eventually receive from it. The face value of the annuity remained the same; the actual buying power of the dollars you would receive has shrunk. Not so with land.

In the case of a good piece of land (or a good stock) where the market value has increased rapidly as a result of people pressure (and purchase pressure on the stock), if you have received *twice* as many dollars worth *half* as much, you may not have made an actual profit in the literal sense but you've got a lot more *buying power* or purchase position than the man who got paid off at the old fixed value with depreciated dollars.

Actually for the small investor the whole inflation hedge smacks a bit of razzle-dazzle. It is impossible to beat inflation. But with well-purchased, well-situated land you can run a dead heat with it and still come out with a good investment dollar. True, you may have to put five quarters together to make that dollar, but the point is—you CAN make it!

Not long ago at the California Real Estate Association convention in Los Angeles, James C. Downs, Jr., a prominent Chicago economist, told the five thousand members present that land is the safest investment the average person can make. "You have heard of someone who suffered a 25 per cent loss in his investments due to a down turn in the stock market," he said, "but who knows of anyone losing 25 per cent of his investment in real estate? It is the most stable commodity available."

Former Secretary of Commerce Luther Hodges has publicly recommended that young Americans go into debt as far as they can afford it in order to invest for their future.

"Don't go into debt beyond your weekly income or monthly income," he cautions, "but go into debt to borrow to invest capital into something."

Putting together the reasoning of these two eminent men, one might well conclude then that it would be sound business practice to go into debt to buy the most stable of all commodities, *good land*.

We could document this sound point of view with literally dozens of statements made by other men of recognized position and ability.

4

A GIANT STEP TOWARD INDEPENDENCE

Now let's take the first step toward finding a successful investment in low-cost, raw, or semideveloped land.

Step One requires you to make a simple decision: For whom should the land investment pay out?—You? Your children? Your grandchildren? That decision may depend somewhat upon your age and your circumstances.

If you are a young couple starting out or a young couple just beginning to get a family established, then quite probably you will want to have your land investment pay out about the time your children will be ready for college. That is most easily done because it gives you the most time for your raw land investment to mature.

If you make your purchase—or begin it—about the time the first child arrives you will have approximately fifteen years in which to make your investment, watch it mature, and cash in on it. At the rate land values are rising in the west it is conceivable that you could cash in on your first investment in half that time and have a second program going well by the time the kids are ready to enter college.

This is not a "how to make a quick million in the western land business without really trying" sort of book; there is no "magic formula," no "hokus pokus," no gizmo or gimmick involved. We are simply trying to show you how we arrived at a successful land investment program. We had to make simple decisions too.

Since we were no longer a young couple just starting out our requirements were a little more complex. We decided that, if possible, we would figure out a program flexible enough to give us a profit within five years and that we would allocate the money from those sales toward the purchase of land for our estate. We felt—and we still do—that, if the children are taken care of in our estate and the land is held in trust, the grandchildren will be taken care of too. Barring unforeseen events that is the way it should work out.

It is always dangerous to generalize, but in this case it seems a reasonable risk; in general, if you are in the twenty- to thirty-year age bracket you should buy at least some of the land for your own profit and some to cover your children's educational expenses. If you are in your thirties, we feel you should also purchase some land for your retirement. If you are in your forties or early fifties, you should be thinking of buying for retirement and your estate. For those of you over fifty-five you should buy for the immediate fun of looking for a good speculation or investment, depending upon whether or not you are in circumstances that will guarantee reasonable security in your old age. Of course you can buy for the grandchildren too. That can be a doubly rewarding investment.

Having decided on your long-range objectives, the next decision to make is how much you can afford to put into a land investment.

Since we are writing this book for persons in the same "moderate circumstances" in which we found ourselves ten years ago, we will not even consider the investments that would be made by a couple who are well fixed. If they are young and well fixed it is probably because someone had the foresight to invest in real estate some years back. It might also be because they are uncommonly sharp, in which case they own real estate, know what we are going to suggest, agree that it works, and therefore do not need to read this book.

We are talking about modest investments that will fit the budget of persons with an average income. At the time of this writing the national average is a little below $5000 per year. If your annual income is somewhat greater than that you can make your land investment program pay out more quickly if you wish. How to do that will be clear in a moment.

If we go back to the principle expounded by Secretary of Commerce Luther Hodges at the end of Chapter Three, the "how much" factor in your investment will be solved automatically by the amount of money you can safely afford to obligate yourself for each month. Certainly it should not be more than you can afford to pay out from current income without jeopardizing the security of your family. Also your ability to pay an obligation should not assume windfalls such as inheritances, raises, or quick profits from other speculations or investments. One of the wisest men we ever knew was a canny little Scotsman named Naylor Rogers. He said, "The most dangerous word in the dictionary is the word 'assume.' Don't assume anything; find out the facts, then act!" "Pop" Rogers practiced what he preached and got the facts. It is no assumption but an incontrovertible fact that he made a pile when his broadcasting interests in Hollywood were sold out to a national radio network in the late thirties. Don't overextend yourself. Know for a fact where you stand. That will determine your credit rating and your risk factor as a borrower. Then go ahead according to a plan.

So—first decide *for whom* the land investment should pay out—then decide *how much* you can afford to put into it. Having done that, you are ready to go looking for the *right* opportunity.

Opportunity does *not* come knocking. But if you go looking for it, armed with the complete description needed to recognize it, then it cannot possibly hide from you . . . even if it turns out to be right under your nose . . . where, by the way, reside most of the opportunities that we mortals miss.

One of the most successful land investors in the west told us not long ago that "nearly all of the good land opportunities are being gobbled up by the outsiders who come into the western states and buy parcels of land right under our noses. Most natives are too close to the parcel to see the progress!" How true that is. Ed Nofziger, whose amusing cartoons and graphs liven up this book, gave us a good example of opportunities missed by nearsighted natives. (For many years Ed drew the famous nearsighted Mr. Magoo.)

"When I was going to U.C.L.A. in 1936," Ed said, "I lived in Sawtelle [adjoining Westwood where the University is located]. Every morning I cut through bean fields from Sepulveda Boulevard, on across Wilshire and up to Westwood Boulevard. There were hundreds of acres of vacant ground there then. I remember a friend of ours telling me that the land was being held too high at fifteen hundred dollars an acre!"

Ed looked a little wistfully in the direction of Los Angeles. "If we'd eaten a few of those beans we could have bought an acre of it. By now we'd have been eating caviar!"

But Ed's older brother was not about to let the outsiders take over right under his nose. In that same year, 1936, he bought a parcel of land in Canoga Park, a suburban community in the Los Angeles area. Ed seems to recall that he paid around six to eight hundred dollars for it. Only twenty-four years later, in 1960, Ed's brother refused an offer of $85,000.

"And the heck of it is," sighed Ed, "he tried to get me to take a piece of it too and that same 'friend' said, 'Don't touch it, boy. It's way overpriced!'"

Sometimes land *is* overpriced, *temporarily*. But later on in this book we'll show you that if you *hold*, as Ed's brother did, the price probably will swing up again and on up and up beyond anything you dreamed of. That's not fiction—that's *fact*.

5

HOW RAW LAND TURNS TO GOLD

Good land is a five letter word spelled W-A-T-E-R. This is most particularly true in the water-short West. But land values depend upon other factors too. Foremost among them is *accessibility*.

This chapter will be the most important one in this book. We have qualified the exactness of our title long since. But if there is such a thing as the *simple* truth about western land (any land!) it is the idea disclosed in these next few pages.

The idea gets more interesting if we take a moment to trace it back to the beginning of our country—back to the days of Jamestown and Plymouth Rock. The same identical concept of growth may be applied to the growth of any country since the very dawn of mankind's history. But only in the past decade has the whole picture of our growth pattern begun to dawn on land development experts, though we are certain that they have used part of the theory more or less consciously for some time.

We've been told often enough that the growth of our country has been willy-nilly, following no predictable pattern, subject to political pressure, economic pressure, and high-pressure sales techniques. This is partly true. But *basically* our country has grown according to an *orderly principle* that has now been analyzed and identified as *the Strip City Theory*.

Like most other truths it is a simple one and once called to our attention it becomes immediately clear—in its entirety.

From the time the first white settlers arrived on this continent the growth of North America has followed a consistent pattern. Ships loaded with immigrants arrived at the newly charted seaports. Settlements were founded there. Most of those ports were large, protected harbors into which navigable rivers emptied. Up those rivers went the more adventurous ones who wished to see what lay beyond their new communities, which soon became towns. A day's voyage up those rivers, they found logical stopping places. They brought others along who liked the frontier's open spaces. Remote villages, hardly more than camps at first, were founded there.

In time, still others came and the villages grew into towns just as the towns at the harbors were busy growing into cities.

Communication between the seaports often was slow and uncertain because of rough weather and the danger of coastal sailing. For quicker, more dependable all-weather communications, post roads were hacked through the wilderness and soon the seaports were connected by land links.

A day's journey along these post roads, inns were established with stables, blacksmith shops, and the other services required by travelers.

Those who provided these services came to live at these stopping places. In time the principal ones became villages and then towns.

Meanwhile the explorers were pushing inland along the rivers and along the valleys the rivers drained. When the explorers reached the point where their sailing craft could no longer buck the currents, they went to lighter, hand-propelled craft and extended their explorations. Other camps were made. When they came to the confluence of two major streams big camps were established. Very quickly these became important towns and cities. Pittsburgh is a prime example. In a hundred years it grew from a frontier fort and trading post to an inland metropolis.

Paralleling these rivers were other post roads. In time explorers found passes, usually via old Indian trails, and made their way through the barrier mountains into adjacent valleys. These trails, soon converted to roads, transported men and goods faster, if not cheaper, than the river craft. When one is claiming an empire, one wants to hurry.

Scouts pushed on, fanning generally westward to the Mississippi Valley, up that vast valley and up its tributary valleys, following the streams that pour into the great central watershed from east and west. And each time, roughly a day's journey from each previous fort or village or town, a new community was established.

Coincidentally with the roads came the network of canals, an ancient transportation system based on the European waterways in the homelands of the many nationalities who were our first citizens.

Then came the first railroads. Almost simultaneously with the development of a practical steam engine by James Watt in 1769, came the development of the locomotive and the steamboat.

We remember Richard Trevithick for the first practical locomotive; and Robert Fulton for the *Clermont*, the first practical steamboat. But there were a half dozen in each field before them.

At first the competition between the railroads and the river craft was bitter. Then, because they were faster and usually could travel the shorter distance between two important points, the railroads gained the upper hand and the steamboat, in the form of the hybrid *Savannah,* turned to the high seas.

Because we must either progress or regress, we cannot stand still, the steamship today is fighting a mortal battle with aircraft; and the railroads, which dominated all transportation for a hundred years, are now engaged in a mortal struggle with the paved road, the throughway, the freeway, the turnpike, the bus, truck, and motor car as well as with the airplane. Whatever the outcome of the individual battle the end result will be complete victory in the relentless war we are waging on the wide-open spaces. Some of us would like to see an armistice declared before the forest primeval has been entirely felled and slashed into siding and shingles and there's no place left for a possum to hide, let alone for a buffalo to roam.

What has caused this great creeping invasion? *People pressure!* We hardly need to include all the census figures that we have spread out before us to prove the point. It is self-evident everywhere you look.

The next question is, which came first, the transportation routes or the travelers who throng them?

Well, in the beginning, of course, the primitive access routes were already there—harbors, rivers, and the open valleys through which they flowed, and the passes over the mountains into still more remote territory.

Then the people came, discovered, and utilized them. Then more people. Up to a point, that is.

There was a leveling-off time as far as the West was concerned, when the eastern and southern and midwestern parts of the country were being consolidated.

But in the mid-nineteenth century, following the Civil War, the population grew restless again. Wars seem to be

mixed blessings. They uproot and displace people who then
see what's on the other side of the mountain. Often they like
what they see or have nothing left to return to, so move on
anyway. Whatever the reason, they move. And people pressure, like any other pressure, tends to exert itself along the
lines of least resistance . . . in this case the most expedient
transport routes.

Impetus is given these migrations by a number of things.
Flights from invasion, flights from compression and poverty
in cities, the search for larger land holdings or more fertile
land and more abundant water, greater stands of timber,
newer, larger, richer mineral deposits, more temperate climate, and, as stated earlier, a relaxation of our own immigration laws in the mid-1800s which opened our land to a
horde of new citizens many of whom tended to seek out
areas similar to their own homelands. As one Middle European immigrant patriarch said to us many years ago, "We
want something different only we like it to be the same."

What he meant, of course, was that he wanted a better
and freer way of life but in an area similar to his native land,
if possible. It was that urge that brought the Spanish, the
Italians, the Basques, the Portuguese, and the Greeks to settle along the California coast. Geographically, there was
much about it that reminded them of home. (It was one such
case history that inspired our current novel, *The Richest Poor
Folks*.)

But often in the history of our growth it has been commercial pressure that has stimulated people pressure. In the beginning, when the first railroads came into the West, rate
wars, free land, and dozens of other inducements were offered to build traffic on the competitive lines. The war between the Santa Fe and Southern Pacific railroads in the
1880s, rumbles of which are still being heard, did more than
anything to stimulate people pressure in the West after the
first great burst of immigration slowed down following the

Gold Rush. The West was going through its second period of consolidation.

Immediately after World War I the country, particularly the West, experienced another population surge. Then came another period of adjustment and consolidation. World War II came. A half-million American men died; three million American babies were born. And each year since, there are more and more. And they grow and marry and produce still more—and more. Whatever else the result may be, prosperity or recession, the end result is people pressure . . . irresistible *people pressure*. And the greatest pressure in this past two decades has been exerted toward the West.

All of this has created a paradox. The cause of this westward migration is pressure and the effect of this pressure is more migration. There is another result, not paradoxical; the pressure, as always, has tended to follow the established lines of transport. It has established a discernible pattern of growth.

But let's go back to the 1800s again for a moment so we can trace the beginning of the pattern clearly.

As people began to pour into the principal population centers and the peripheral areas began to fill up, the little out-pressing streams were diverted by natural obstacles . . . mountains, rivers, and seacoasts. People pressure backed up and population growth was forced out along the main roads.

In cases where a city and a town were reasonably close (in the eastern seaboard states they all were) the out-pressing streams of people met and joined. Solid suburban settlements grew up on either side of the main roads and filled in the adjacent areas.

As the nation's population grew in other regions the same process took place. Adjacent towns became suburbs and in time suburbs became urbanized, made a part of the main city. Soon a metropolitan area could be seen forming. It appeared as a high-density civic center at the hub of a series of strip communities radiating outward along the main roads. Blocked by the Alleghenies on the west and the Atlantic on the east, the oldest part of our country soon developed into a series of such strips of population. At first they were not all joined. But with the great increase in population and with the development of the new high-speed interurban transport it was soon possible to see that eventually all of the coastal cities would be joined in one great strip city to which we have given the graphic name, "Megaloctopus."

If you remember the story of R.B.'s 100-acre farm in Ohio, you'll have a fine microcosmic example of the evolution of a city. Put two or more such cities within easy reach of one another and soon they have evolved into a strip city. The process is simple. It is also interesting and it would not take much persuasion to get us to do an extensive "in depth" study of the history of our country's growth for it would also be a history of our country's greatness. It will continue to be such an inspiring history unless we suddenly begin to abuse our greatest natural resource, our precious available land.[1]

It doesn't take a graduate economist to see that as people become more numerous and need more and more room, the one vital commodity, land, (of which there is a forever-fixed amount) becomes more and more in demand. And as with any commodity, the balance between demand and supply determines value. Spell the rest of the land value story out for yourself. It's as simple as A-B-C!

Now, if you read the literature sent out by some land developers you might well be led to believe that ANY piece of western land should be grabbed up immediately . . . most

---

[1] In Chapter Thirteen, "Into the Future via the Past," we have included some frightening predictions just released in a "Resources for the Future" survey. We say "frightening" despite the fact that the survey seems based on a common-sense projection.

APPROXIMATE AREAS EMBRACED BY
STRIP CITIES AND ISLANDS

SEATTLE
SPOKANE
PORTLAND
EUGENE
BOISE
WELCOME TO OUR
FAIR STRIP CITIES
SACRAMENTO
RENO
CARSON
CITY
SALT LAKE CITY
SAN FRANCISCO
DENVER
COLORADO
SPRINGS
LAS
VEGAS
SANTA FE
ALBUQUERQUE
WE'RE
NEXT! L.A.
PHOENIX
SAN DIEGO
TUCSON

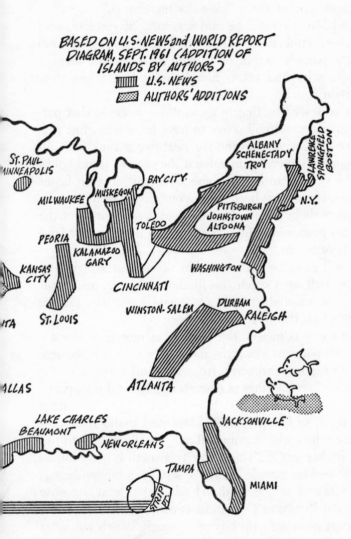

BASED ON U.S.NEWS and WORLD REPORT
DIAGRAM, SEPT. 1961 (ADDITION OF
ISLANDS BY AUTHORS)

||||| U.S. NEWS
▒▒▒ AUTHORS' ADDITIONS

ST. PAUL
MINNEAPOLIS

MILWAUKEE   MUSKEGON   BAY CITY

ALBANY
SCHENECTADY
TROY
LAWRENCE
SPRINGFIELD
BOSTON

PEORIA   KALAMAZOO   TOLEDO   PITTSBURGH   N.Y.
         GARY   JOHNSTOWN
KANSAS   ALTOONA
CITY
                 CINCINNATI   WASHINGTON
ST. LOUIS
TA
              WINSTON-SALEM   DURHAM
                               RALEIGH

DALLAS

                               ATLANTA

LAKE CHARLES   JACKSONVILLE
BEAUMONT
              NEW ORLEANS
                        TAMPA
                    STRIP
                      ITY   MIAMI

particularly theirs. You might be led to take as "gospel" the story that originated with us when we told of our first encounter with one of these "blue-sky merchants."

"Mr. and Mrs. Cooley," he said urgently, "if you kin stand on that there land 'thout fallin' off, buy it!" Judging from some of the parcels he showed us with SOLD signs on them, a lot of folks who had taken him literally had taken their lives in their hands.

It may very well be that in generations to come that particular man's counsel will prove to have been wise. But personally we can't worry beyond the next two generations. *All* western land will increase in value if the present trend holds. That is the simple truth. But some areas will develop faster than others. If we have been stating our case clearly in these pages then perhaps you are beginning to get a glimpse of the pattern that determines the formula for finding the *best* land for your investment.

If you will examine the maps that illustrate the strip city theory you will soon catch the fundamental picture of our country's phenomenal growth. Once you have that picture clearly in mind, the rest will be easy.

The strip city is merely the modern extension of the ancient growth patterns along the natural lines of communication and transport. Parkways, freeways, and turnpikes now have become "natural lines of communication and transport," though at the five o'clock rush hour a poor commuter caught in the bumper to bumper, smog-blanketed snail's pace procession may feel like arguing about the word, "natural."

As one broker put it, "The strip city growth is good for investors but bad for people." How he separates human beings into investors and people we didn't ask. But at least one state governor, Pat Brown of California, is concerned with people in the fastest growing strip city of them all, which will soon reach from San Diego to San Francisco. Governor Brown wants legislation to put an end to the willy-nilly incorporation of suburbs into cities with all of their duplication of services and uncoordinated zoning laws. Such legislation is mandatory if this tremendous rate of growth is not to cause us to fall and be crushed beneath the compounding economic problems we are creating for ourselves, problems whose temporary solutions are too often sought in an increased tax load —at every level.

But the legislation needed to bridle this runaway development of open land—this horde of homeseekers racing to the outskirts so quickly that soon an area once called "outskirts" will be remembered only by the oldest inhabitants—will have to be discussed by others more expert than we. We are concerned here merely with describing the nature of people pressure, its effect on the growth of communities—particularly in the West—and the effect of that growth on raw and semi-developed land values.

It must be obvious that even in the growth patterns of these ribbons of urban development snaking out along new highways there is still a clear-cut need to pick and choose the sort of opportunity that fits your purse and your time plan. You can't just run out and nail down the first piece of vacant land you see that lies outside the city limits and then confidently wait for the thundering herd of buyers to rush up to you in an attempt to outbid one another. It doesn't happen that fast. But it happens a lot faster than most people think it does *if* they happen to own land in the path of an identifiable strip city.

Actually the anatomy of a growing community in the strip-city era is much the same as the anatomy of the growth of the semi-isolated metropolis of decades past. There is still the concentric growth from city hall, so to speak, with the city radiating outward where space permits. There is still the progression from urban to suburban to agricultural to raw land. And to that, of course, must be added recreational land too.

It is just that these peripheral, less thickly settled suburban and agricultural areas now tend to follow along the outer edges or margins of the strips through the centers of which run the main highways.

We can remember when there were mainly open fields and farms in the areas between San Francisco and San Jose and between San Diego and Los Angeles . . . or for that matter, between Hollywood, Beverly Hills, and Culver City, and between downtown Los Angeles and Long Beach, and in Arizona between Phoenix and Scottsdale, to name just a few.

The lucky farmers who owned acreage midway between these urban points found themselves being squeezed by people pressure from both sides. They discovered also that from being caught in the squeeze of our "Megaloctopus," they could get very, very rich indeed . . . even after taxes. In a way, the happy plight of the farmers illustrates the fundamental principle involved in finding your own investment or speculative land. The trick is to get squeezed by a Megaloctopus; the trick is to be there when the bean and the potato fields are cut up into industrial parcels and city lots and the light industries and rows of nearly identical tract houses are built with all of the usual fanfare and hullabaloo. The next thing to come along will be the shopping center. Around this area will grow another complex of service businesses. In time this new community will become a microcosmic city. And in very little more time it will be incorporated and begin to function as such.

Now there are three cities in a row—the two original, widely separated ones and the third city that grew midway between them and spread out around its starting point on the new highway or freeway. We perceive the evolutionary pattern again: raw to agricultural to industrial to adjacent residential with a shopping and service complex located in the areas designated by the subdividers as C-zoned or commercially zoned property. In this case the only difference between the giant and the pygmy is in the number of cells in each; the anatomy is identical. And where communities are concerned, the pygmy can grow into a giant and merge with the adjacent giants to form a super-gigantic strip city or megalopolis. And, as the map shows, that's exactly what's happening in thirteen major areas of the United States today.

6

THE FIVE TYPES OF INVESTMENT LAND

There are five main types of investment land and all five exist in, or in the vicinity of, or in the eventual path of a growing strip city. They are:

> Urban land
> Suburban land
> Farm land
> Raw land
> Recreational land

Let's discuss briefly the differences in these lands as we see them and attempt to classify them as speculations or investments.

First of all, a solid lead-pipe cinch of a piece of super-expensive real estate can become a speculation of the most dangerous order if one attempts to buck a trend or lead by too far a trend in any particular area.

There are some people who will tell you that once upon a time the Empire State Building was such a speculation. Certainly its history seems to have been stormy enough. Some people have told us that this was because the original backers built it at the wrong time and in the wrong place. We don't know whether or not that was an accurate observation. But we do know that business offices tended to build north from Forty-second Street instead of south toward Thirty-fourth Street, where the tallest, most exciting building in the world stands.

But whatever the truth about that particular piece of real estate, it does seem that on a high-density island such as Manhattan—and with time working in its favor—the question can only be an academic one. If there was ever a major city where people pressure eventually will demand every inch of living and working space it is New York and most particularly the Borough of Manhattan. So, if there was a problem it was only temporary—one of timing. Often then, *timing* can make the difference between investment and speculation.

First, let's define the words speculation and investment: Webster's New Collegiate Dictionary says of speculation, ". . . to enter into a transaction or venture the profits of which are conjectural or subject to chance; specif., to buy or sell with the expectation of profiting by fluctuations in price."

The same source defines investment this way: ". . . the investing of money or capital for income or profit . . ."

Quite literally there is an element of speculation in most investments. Inversely most speculations are investments of an uncertain order.

For our purposes we would like to define the word speculation as meaning an investment in land in which there is an element of uncertainty as to exactly *when and how much* the parcel will increase in value. The greater the element of uncertainty the cheaper the land and the greater the element of speculation.

We would like to define investment as applied to raw or semideveloped land as meaning a sum of money spent to purchase a parcel of land on which it is reasonable to predict, by means of the evidence usually employed by realtors, banks, and other interested parties, approximately *when* one can safely expect the parcel to increase in value and, within reason, by what amount.

There is no hard and fast rule. The land we purchased at Fire Island Pines ten years ago was called a "rank speculation" by our practical-minded business manager. Five years later, he conceded it had been a "hell of a good *investment!*"

There must be as many such examples as there are parcels of land that have been bought and sold in this country. Sometimes we're tempted to just cut through all the doubletalk and say simply, *An investment is a speculation on which you guessed right.* But that wouldn't be entirely correct either. So perhaps the most accurate thing to say is this: An investment is a purchase which *thorough research* (and intuition) tells you will increase in value within the period of time you have set for maturity. If that period of time lies within say five to ten years because the pressure in the immediate area indicates a fairly quick increase in value, then that expenditure might well be called a land investment.

If careful research—and again, intuition—indicates the growth may take longer than ten years (we're talking about undeveloped or partially improved land, remember) then we'd say call it a *speculative investment.* Price is an element in defining the nature of the purchase too. If, as is the case with many of these raw-land desert ranchos, you are buying your 1¼ or 2½ acres at a price which is hundreds of times the assessed value of the land, then friend, in our opinion, you are speculating and there's no quibbling about terminology! But let us show you how dangerous it is to draw hard and fast conclusions.

We have a letter carrier named Al Cook who delivers

mail here on our hill overlooking the Pacific Ocean in Laguna Beach, California. Al is a wonderful young man, an
ex-Marine. It takes an ex-Marine to lug forty pounds of mail
up these hills afoot! In fact we think the Postmaster General
should have special medals struck for our Laguna Beach letter carriers. They are the climbingest, smilingest postal employees we know.

Ordinarily Al doesn't say very much beyond the usual
amenities. But not long ago he was moved to ask a discreet
question after he had lugged a short ton of land promoters'
brochures to us during nearly a year of research. He finally
broke down and wanted to know if we were going to buy
some desert land.

"Well, we own quite a bit already, Al," we replied, "but
if you know of any exceptional buys we're always interested
in listening."

He blinked a bit and then said, almost shyly, "I bought a
piece in Lake Mojave Ranchos outside of Kingman, Arizona."

Before Al Cook knew what had happened to him he was
in the dining nook having coffee. We had caught a "live one"
and we weren't about to let him get away without a quizzing.
Ours is the last stop on his route so we didn't feel too guilty
about tampering with the U.S. mail.

In a matter of minutes we got these answers to these questions and, in the process, some valuable insight into the attitude of many of the customers who have purchased land in
these controversial desert developments.

Q: When did you buy?
A: In 1960.
Q: How much land did you buy?
A: One parcel—one and one-eighth acres.
Q: Do you mind telling us how much you paid for it?
A: No, I don't mind . . . I paid $495. It's gone up to $695
now. [A few days later Al dropped by to say it had gone
up to $895.]

Q: Did you see the land before you purchased?

A: No . . . but I could have.

Q: What persuaded you to buy there?

A: My uncle has land in the same development.

Q: (sneakily) Misery loves company, eh?

A: (amiably) No . . . he's very well satisfied.

Q: What about you? Have you seen your land yet?

A: Yes . . . I saw it last spring.

Q: Were you disappointed?

A: No . . . not really.

Q: What was your primary reason for buying?

A: Speculation . . . a place to go . . . to get away from home for a change. It's a good place to camp out in a trailer if you want to.

Q: Do you intend to live there someday?

A: I haven't decided yet. [Al looks to be in his late twenties so it's not surprising that he'd be undecided about retirement!]

Q: Will your postal retirement pay keep you and your family there if you should want to move to Arizona someday?

A: Yes . . . I think so.

Q: Would you expect to supplement your income?

A: Yes. I'm taking a course in sign painting from I.C.S.

Q: Do you think your rancho will prove to be a sound investment in time?

A: Well, I said I paid $495 for it and it's $695 now so it's gone up $200 in about two years.

Q: The company arbitrarily raised the prices though didn't they?

A: Yes . . .

Q: Could you sell your rancho for $695 now?

A: I believe so. [As of August 1, 1967, it is worth $1000]

1   Above, one of the new citrus orchards planted in the Mesa Grande section of Rancho California. To date 6000 acres have been purchased for agricultural purposes, mostly by growers forced to leave metropolitan areas because of urban asphalt, smog and skyrocketing taxes.   *(McKoon Photography, Costa Mesa)*

2   California City's recreation area, August 1967. Five years ago we watched bulldozers begin work here. Now there is a lake, a fine golf course, a new motel, apartment house complexes, a small boat marina and an ultra-modern indoor recreation center—developer's promises—all kept! A growing city lies to lower left, out of picture.   *(Joseph Jasgur, Hollywood)*

3 "Graded roads" to home sites on a typical rancho-type subdivision in the Southwest desert country. Power lines in distance serve only a small percentage of the sites. There are no water lines, no telephones, no sewers, not even controlled storm drains. A flash flood had wiped out the "avenue" in the foreground! This is the sort of subdivision we mean when we say "it is conveniently located in the heart of West Hellangone!"

4 The tangled skein of freeways converging on downtown Los Angeles. The Division of Highways maps which project the needs of the western states to about 1980 show that this is only the beginning! (*Photo by State of California Department of Public Works Division of Highways*)

5   Hollywood, California, from the head of Gower Street at the turn of the century. The orchards and hayfields in the distance were planted over acres destined to sprout oil wells. These in turn gave way to residences and now high-rise office buildings and apartments.   (*Photo by Title Insurance and Trust Company, Los Angeles, Collection of Historical Photographs*)

6   The same view of Hollywood only three decades later, in 1930. By 1960 all of the open lots in the foreground had been built upon and many of the older houses in the foreground (Franklin Ave.) had been razed and replaced by high-rise apartment buildings.   (*Photo by Title Insurance and Trust Company, Los Angeles, Collection of Historical Photographs*)

7 (*From file copies of the San Fernando Valley Times TODAY*)

8 In 1927 the Ventura State Highway was a "new" two-lane, paved road. By 1964 it had become the Ventura Freeway, an eight-lane, high-speed highway that reaches from San Diego to Santa Barbara. The area is a high-density strip city, part of the Los Angeles "megaloctopus." If you visit this site today, bring your own walnuts! (*From file copies of the San Fernando Valley Times TODAY*)

9   The All-American Canal carrying precious Colorado River water to California's Imperial Valley. This . . .

10   on this . . .

11   equals THIS! A view of a square mile (640 acres) of row crops on an Imperial Valley farm just twenty minutes from Calexico and Mexicali on the Baja border.

TWO MORE MAJOR HIGHWAYS

S. P. PASSENGER SERVICE LOOMS

ANOTHER MAIN CORNER IS SOLD

ACREAGE GOES INTO BUSINESS, INCOME LOTS | **VALLEY DRY CLEANING PLANT TO BE ERECTED HERE**

NEW INDUSTRY IN NO. SECTION

TUJUNGA DAM SEEMS NEARER
TWO AIRPORT SITES NOW BEING CONSIDERED BY CITY

BUILDING TOTAL PASSES MILLION

GREAT VALLEYS COOPERATING

12   The classic pattern of progress! In 1927 this was almost open country. Today this is the *very heart* of the Los Angeles megalopolis. These reproductions of headlines were taken from the files of the *San Fernando Valley Times TODAY* — the daily newspaper that has so long served this area. The San Fernando Valley (with the exception of Burbank and the town of San Fernando) is part of the City of Los Angeles. The valley area is "home" for 942,000 people now. By 1982 it is estimated a million and a half people will live here! When these papers were printed we used to hunt jack rabbits in the area. Now, taken as a city, it is larger than Cleveland, contributes more to the space program than any other area in the nation and is ranked in the top ten markets in buying power. Its retail sales also rank in the top ten. Pretty good for a land-promotion scheme that had been picked to fail — because it was too far from Los Angeles!

13 Del Webb's Sun City near Phoenix, Arizona, in 1959. It lies in heart of prime agricultural area served by the Salt River Project.   (*Photo by Arizona Development Board*)

14 Sun City four years later. Two more such senior-citizen communities have been developed by Del Webb in Southern California. One is in Kern County near Bakersfield and one is near Riverside. Other new ones are springing up in the heart of once rich agricultural areas all over the West. They exert a tremendous effect on the value of adjacent acreage.   (*Photo by Arizona Development Board*)

15, 16, 17   The San Francisco "megaloctopus" caught in the act of squeezing an artichoke farm in nearby San Mateo County. Dramatic proof of the encroachment of residential development on existing farms. *People Pressure* soon makes the land itself worth more to the farmer than the crops he can raise on it.

Top Photo: The original artichoke farms in December of 1954 before Linda Mar in San Mateo County, California, became a fashionable seaside residential development.

Middle Photo: The same area a few months later.

Bottom Photo: The development completed the following year. *(Photos by the Advance Star and Green Sheet, Burlingame, Cal.)*

Q: What modern conveniences are available at your parcel now?

A: Well, there aren't any paved streets yet . . . at least not on my property and the nearest water is six miles . . . and the electricity is six miles too. We could use bottled gas; everybody does there. There are no sewers . . . you dig a cesspool.

As of August 1967, there is still no water system, no sewer system and no natural gas. However, a sizable community named Dolan Springs has grown up with a post office, paved streets, power and a chamber of commerce. There is also a recreation center serving residents of an increasing number of homes, many of the latter in the $15,000–$20,000 bracket. Several more expensive ones are building.

Excellent medical facilities are available in Kingman, Arizona, about thirty miles distant. A bus service takes students to and from elementary and high schools.

Q: How far are you from Highway 93? [The main road from Las Vegas to Kingman.]

A: My property is twelve miles from the highway.

Q: When you purchased by mail, Al, did you get a full description of the property?

A: Yes, I did. When I sent my deposit I got the full disclosure paper the State of California makes them fill out before they can sell here. [California was the pioneer in this protection for out-of-state land purchasers. New, tougher laws require accurate, detailed descriptions of land and existing improvements. Penalties are stiff.]

Q: Was it accurate?

A: I would say so, yes. Anyway, when I sent in my ten-dollar deposit I could have gotten my money back if I didn't like the deal.

Q: But you *did* like it. How about your neighbors?

A: None of them are complaining. They're enjoying it up to the hilt.

And so they were, so far as we could tell. Before the conversation with Al Cook we had visited his development. It's true, we didn't talk to a single person who was unhappy at the comparative isolation or the sometimes primitive living.

As one friendly gent at the little service station said, "Folks, if you had come from a cold-water flat in Brooklyn, this would look like paradise to you!"

Well, since one of us did come from a flat in Brooklyn (with hot water, however) we understood what he meant. But we personally know a lot of flat dwellers in Brooklyn who, if faced with the prospect of so much wide open space, would run and hide in the nearest subway. It is largely a state of mind. We must say that Al and those neighbors of his that we had talked to had the proper state of mind for pioneering in the Arizona desert. It is a beautiful land, if you have the eyes to see it. And none of them seemed to be too concerned with the fact that the much advertised lake was quite a few miles away. And why should they, really, when Los Angelenos hitch up their boat trailers and travel nearly three hundred miles round trip to fish and water ski for a short weekend on the Salton Sea? Lake Mojave, Lake Mead, and Lake Havasu are a lot closer than that to Al's rancho!

Though this observation may not properly belong right here, we can't resist saying that it seems to us that a lot of writers who have journeyed west to look and laugh at some of these ranchos have not exactly been playing fair with land dividers as a whole. Sure, it makes a sensational feature to set up a card table in the middle of the desert and decorate it with a silver candelabra and a champagne bucket and sit forlornly in the broiling sun in the middle of "West Hellangone." It's a funny picture. But it is not entirely a true representation. After seven thousand miles of going through these subdivisions we feel we've seen as much of them as any other writers.

We confess we saw some pretty "raw" developments which were not as advertised . . . and we saw a buzzard sitting on a street sign marked Park Ave. and Forty-second St.

We think some of the older people who have purchased these deals sight unseen have been taken if they think they're going to be able to live comfortably there or make a profit out of a resale before their great-grandchildren are ready for college. But the really bad deals were few and far between. And there's plenty of precedent to show that a few decades from now they might well have turned out to be a "hell of a good investment" too.

Since this book is not intended to substitute for a formal course in real estate, let's use that dangerous word "assume" again and say that you know by now that it is difficult to accurately define the subtle differences between an investment and a speculation for there are too many factors involved, not the least of which is your own attitude toward what you buy. One man's speculation is another man's investment . . . as is the case of Al Cook and his neighbors in Arizona.

More and more is being done, as we said earlier, to prevent unscrupulous land dividers from bilking the public. New laws are being passed, old laws beefed up, and there is a general and determined awakening to the danger in the land sales racket so far as local, state, and federal authorities are concerned. But they have never yet been able to pass a law to protect a dedicated damned fool from himself. So we can safely assume that in the future, as in the past, the swindlers will find a way to accommodate the suckers who insist upon being swindled.

To sum up this chapter let's go back to the five types of investment and speculation land in or around the growing strip cities.

It must be clear that the urban land is the most expensive and we'll rule it out of the discussion here because it is the most highly developed land in the world and subject to a special and very complicated set of rules and regulations. We know very little about this sort of property and if, as, and when we get involved in it you may be certain the best insurance we can buy will be the services of the best realtor we can find—and the most knowledgeable lawyer. Realtors, by the way, are forbidden by their code of ethics to render legal opinions or to function in areas properly reserved for legal specialists. Most of them, however, are extremely well informed in the matter of laws affecting their sphere of operation and their opinions, however informal, are usually dependable.

Suburban land is the next category as we move outward from city hall, the nerve center of our metropolis (which is getting to be part of a megalopolis). Most of you own land in the suburbs . . . and have your own homes on it, so you know the relative problems of valuing a house and a lot as an investment. Generally, if you are in a "good section" your investment is as "good as gold" and in time you'll sell out for a profit and have had your rent free for years too. Or at worst you'll sell for enough to pay out the mortgage and have a bundle of "fighting money" besides.

If you live in a big city you've probably seen commercial encroachment on the older areas and, in turn, this may have given way to light industrial. Unhappily some neighborhoods, usually the older ones, get run down and become "tenamentized." The equally unhappy fact is, though, that even this property can often be a lucrative investment for the landlords. And sometimes those run-down neighborhoods get revived quite unexpectedly. In nearly every big city in the nation there are examples of that. Los Angeles' remarkable Bunker Hill project is an outstanding example.

In the mid-1940s we could have purchased a half block of

run-down tenement houses in mid-Manhattan, on Second
Ave. The price? $80,000. Today there is a high-rise building
on those lots. They sold for better than $2,000,000 in 1959.
We know now that we should have bought them. Along
about Chapter Eleven we'll tell you the story of those two
sad characters, I. Hadda and I. Coulda!

Farmland comes next. And if it is definitely in the path of
a strip city's progress and still priced within reason, it is
among the best investments you can make. But you'll have
to be prepared to hold it for a while and see that good use is
made of it in the meantime. We think there is something im-
moral about sitting on once productive land that might still
be earning a living for somebody, even on a share basis. At
least it should be making its taxes.

There is some farmland in the San Fernando Valley area
of Los Angeles that we could have purchased less than
twenty years ago for $500 an acre. Today, if they would sell
(most large holdings find it necessary in time because of rising taxes) the land would price at $50,000 an acre and more.
Yes, in less than twenty years! In every major area of the
West the story is the same.

Some pages back we told you about giving a talk at the
Los Angeles Ebell Club. That was the day we met a woman
who had just become a millionairess, that very morning!
How? She had gone into escrow on farmland that her hus-
band had bought in Encino twenty-three years earlier—for
$500 an acre. She had sold 100 acres of it for $3,000,000. She
looked very happy to us . . . and quite young and very attractive. No wonder! Those who know say there's nothing
like a brisk rubdown with a crisp, new million-dollar bill to
rejuvenate you.

The "beauty part" of these success stories—R.B.'s included
—is that most of these fortunate people never ever in their
wildest dreams expected to make so much money from their
old patch of land.

Sudden wealth will not come as such a surprise to the young people of the next generation if they set about investing or speculating according to the principles outlined in this book and, as we always caution, do it by counseling with experts in the field.

Now we are at raw land. As you have deduced by following the obvious strip-city theory . . . it lies well out beyond the urban and suburban land but not necessarily beyond the good farmland. For instance, in Southern California's Antelope Valley and in Arizona's Paradise Valley and in most other areas surrounding the principal cities of the western states you can still find good raw land practically adjacent to operating farms.

There's an interesting situation about raw land that is developing as a result of people pressure: As the demand for suburban housing grows, the demand for good, flat land grows too. Very soon the builders bid up the price of level, easily buildable land to the point where farmers cannot resist taking their capital gains and running. As a result the vitally needed farms are being driven farther and farther out into the wide-open spaces (where water is available, of course) with the further result that inexpensive raw land is quickly being changed into expensive farmland. If the process of evolution continues . . . and it certainly will in the paths of these strip cities . . . the farmland will again be bid up to the point where the subdividers will get it and the farmers will be on the move again.

Cavett Robert, who was at that time assistant real estate commissioner for the state of Arizona, pointed out that we may well have to come to a day of reckoning as they did in Europe. "Over there," he said, "they built their cities on the untillable hills and saved their precious level land for agriculture. It certainly seems more sensible than doing what we're in the process of doing to our most fertile western farmland."

He pointed to a huge housing development. "Those houses are standing on 1200 acres of the finest agricultural land in Arizona. Somehow that doesn't make sense in the long run."

We agree. But we can take heart; with new earth-moving techniques the hilly land once again is getting to be the most desirable for homesites. Maybe relief is coming in the shape of the relentless bulldozer and skip loader. Who knows? Another possibility, of course, is that communities will tend to grow vertically. There are some interesting possibilities in this skyward trend. But personally we feel that in the long run, for the average small investor, the marginal land on the periphery of the strip cities is the best buy.

The last of the five categories is recreational land. This should take the least explanation since it is obviously land in or adjacent to areas where one may indulge in out-of-door activities of various sorts. Generally speaking it falls into two classes, the developed subdivisions in the vicinity of large bodies of water open to the public, and semideveloped or undeveloped acreage lying within easy driving distance of hunting, fishing, and skiing areas. The California–Nevada–Lake Tahoe area is a fine example. The Idaho lake country is one of many others.

Recreational land is most often found at some distance from the centers of population that will merge into the eventual megalopolis. But broadly speaking the same fundamental principles apply in seeking it out for investment or speculation as apply in finding farm and raw land. In the chapter coming up now, we'll begin to outline specifically the methods used to locate and evaluate such property.

7

HOW TO GET SQUEEZED BY A "MEGALOCTOPUS"

So far we've seen enough of the basic growth pattern of the modern strip city to recognize its beginnings on an ordinary road map. But in order to confirm *all* of the localized directions of growth we have found it very useful to dig out old maps of the same areas and see how many new communities and new roads have been added in the intervening years.

If you compare 1950 and 1960 maps of almost any urban region in the United States, you'll be astounded at the amount of growth. The census figures state it clearly but the maps make much more dramatic and graphic evidence. If you want a real jolt, go back another ten years and dig out a 1940 map from the library. A fine source, by the way, is the back file of *National Geographic* magazines. That remarkable publication is one of the greatest living historical documents on earth . . . beyond being one of the pleasantest things that can happen to you in a doctor's office. Its maps are superb.

In fact, with the automobile clubs, the oil companies, and what-not, no people on earth have it so good. We Americans are the most map-happy citizens in the world.

After you've looked at the maps and done a little comparing, get in the family car and drive around the periphery of your city. Better take a sandwich; you'll be later than you think.

Unless you happen to be a teamster and are constantly exploring your city with a truckload of something, you'll find areas that will surprise you, even if you think you know your home town. Subdivisions, tracts, shopping centers, out-door theaters, golf courses, parks, playgrounds, and what-not spring up so fast these days that you simply lose track of them. But don't lose track of this one point: *Every one of those new developments stands on acreage that once was inexpensive.* Often it was considered worthless but, nonetheless, it probably made a rich man out of the owner who had the good fortune or good sense to hold it long enough.

Not long ago we were visiting the beautiful Beverly Hills home of comedian Ken Murray and his delightful wife, Bette Lou. Ken was giving us a preview of his second candid "home movie" feature called, "Hollywood Without Make-up."

Ginger Rogers' name came up and Ken, who is filled with a wealth of wonderful anecdotes, hauled the ever-present cigar out of his mouth and said, "Ginger was one of the really smart stars. She invested most of her money in land." He thought for a moment, then grinned. "You know, she has a pretty crazy formula for finding a good investment. She drives out beyond the city limits sign, buys vacant land, then waits for them to move the sign on beyond her."

Actually Ginger and her mother, Lela, have gone well beyond the city limits of Hollywood. Several years back when Ginger was appearing on "The Perry Como Show" for us, we sat with her in Bergdorf-Goodman's on Fifth Ave. while she was being fitted for some gowns. Strangely enough, most of the idle conversation that afternoon centered around our respective ranches . . . our own former Face Rock Ranch in Washington's Methow Valley and her place in the Rogue River Valley in Oregon. Both regions would qualify as among the most beautiful on earth—both are in the process of being "discovered" for their investment possibilities. And we must confess, as lovers of the unspoiled out-of-doors, that in a way we're sorry. But, as early as it is in these areas—and in many others throughout the West—already people holding land are finding that values are going up, especially if they are on, or adjacent to, the main lines of communication.

But to get back to the comparison of maps and the exploration trip around your city, if you'll do that to get the general "lay of the land," then plan some additional trips to specific areas that look promising, you'll soon begin to form your own mental map of the population flow. If one could accelerate the process like Walt Disney does in his fantastic stop-motion movies of flowers blooming, the strip-city population flow would probably look like a great, slow-moving blob of heavy oil spreading out along the paths of least resistance, finally channeling its main flow along the "grooves" that are the roads, freeways, and railroads. You don't see the spreading process from day to day . . . but you see it with astonishing clearness when you take periodic trips.

Nowhere was this demonstrated more dramatically than in the State of Hawaii. When we approached the Honolulu Airport in mid-January of 1967 we were stunned by the postwar change! Swamps had been filled in. Waikiki Beach looked like Miami Beach turned the other way. Rows of luxury high-rise resort hotels stood wall-to-wall from the Aloha Tower to Diamond Head. (In this revised edition we discuss land investment possibilities in the Hawaiian Islands in the section labeled "Supplement.")

We feel it is permissible to use the word "assume" if you

use it this way: Let's assume now that you have made your preliminary and secondary exploratory trips around your own metropolis and that you have found an area that you feel might interest you. Your "feel" for an area can be an important part of your investment too. Often a person whose feelings for an area are negative will overlook things happening right under his nose, get discouraged, and sell out too soon, missing the fabulous profits he might have made. "Feel" or enthusiasm for your investment is an intangible perhaps, but quite literally it is one of the most important determinants; but it should spring from a strong conviction based on good information. Don't discount it and don't let some high-pressure land pusher "push you into a deal" that goes against your grain, even though the facts seem properly represented. If you are really "sold" on an area your enthusiasm will help sell others. Convincing word-of-mouth publicity is one of the most potent value boosters in the land business. But again—it must be based on *facts*. So try to pick an area you can honestly "talk up" with all of your heart.

Back to our assumption: You are now interested in an area. The next thing to do is to pick a licensed broker or realtor. Drop in and talk to him. He's "sold" or he wouldn't be operating in the area. Listen to what he has to say . . . get some typical prices for semideveloped and raw land. Then visit several others and ask them questions too. Although they are all sold on the same general area, no two brokers see the same land identically. Each will have something to add and the more you learn about land the more you'll *want* to learn about it. It is fascinating.

Don't be timid about dropping in. Real estate men will welcome you as an interested party. And they'll take their chances on being good enough at their profession to sell you. Be honest with them; don't mislead them; state your purpose candidly. Even if he doesn't see you again, a smart broker knows that the "lookers" have come to him because interest has been generated in the area. From you he will find out how. That can help him. Also, a reputable realtor will be the first to admit that an investment land purchase is probably the second most important investment you'll ever make in your lifetime. (Your home comes first.) He will recognize the need for compatibility between the realtor and the customer in so important a matter. The first impression you get of an area is apt to be from the real estate men you talk with during the exploratory phase of your search. First impressions are mighty important. Realtors understand this too . . . they are not like traveling salesmen who sell you something then grab the next bus. The realtor sells you, then lives next door to you. He wants a happy neighbor because, if he's pleased you, your word of mouth may well bring him more business. Most of us can't resist sharing a good deal with a friend. And, because we're human, perhaps we should add, *when* there's enough to go around.

Now then, in order to eliminate undesirable land and narrow down the field of selection to the best piece for you, there are some questions you should ask these real estate men.

We are going to give you the basic questions in a moment. But bear in mind that each question may suggest other questions along the same line that will produce still added information. As usual you must use common sense. There is no magic formula that works infallibly in all cases for all buyers. Only fundamental principles come close to doing that . . . and that's the real concern of this book.

If profit is your primary motive the thing you'll need to know before making an investment in land is whether or not your intended purchase lies within or adjacent to an area that seems certain to develop within the time period you have arbitrarily set for the maturing of your investment.

This is repetitious, we know. But these fundamentals need to be repeated until you have made them a part of your basic thinking. The all-important questions about the *purpose* of your investment must become automatic . . . it is your first line of defense against high-pressure salesmanship and the possibility of wasting your money on something you don't really want.

"If profit is your primary motive," we said. But sometimes profit can be just an extra-added attraction. If your primary motive is to find land for a home and perhaps a small self-sustaining farm (it pays its taxes and expenses), then that is your primary motive; the profit motive, if, as, and when you decide to sell is secondary. However, since in most cases the profit motive is the primary one, we are going to use it as the basis for the specific guides set down in these next few pages.

We are against defacing books (most books, that is!) but if you must, cut these questions out and take them with you. Better still, copy the questions in upcoming Chapter Eight. *Best of all, take this book with you.* The related photographs have been carefully chosen to help you compare the areas you are interested in with areas that have already begun to develop. The similarities will be striking . . . and we hope very helpful too!

8

THIRTEEN LUCKY QUESTIONS

After searching through dozens of books and papers, talking to literally scores of brokers, salesmen, and realtors; after interviewing the real estate commissioners and assistant commissioners of the states in which the bulk of the raw land promotions are located; after talking to Better Business bureaus, to real estate lawyers, bankers, chamber of commerce groups, development board heads, and countless others, including persons who bought land for speculation or investment, the most complete set of "safe-guides"—as we call them—still seems to be that prepared by the National Better Business Bureau, Inc. of 230 Park Ave., New York.

In a brochure entitled *Real Estate Promotions* the National Better Business Bureau outlines thirteen points upon which a customer should be entirely satisfied before making a purchase. While these "safe-guides" deal primarily with lots and the sort of real estate transactions generally known as "promotions," which often involve improved or semi-improved land, they also apply admirably to raw land parcels. Quite often such land will have no basic conveniences within miles of it. It is important to know that . . . and to know how far distant they are, how much it will cost when they do become available, who pays for them, and *when* they are likely to become available. These factors determine the relative value of land at any given time. A short distance away identical land may be worth hundreds of dollars an acre more because of the immediate availability of improvements and utilities.

This checking up is the hardest work you'll have to do. But we have found that it can be made far easier and more accurate by enlisting the services of a reputable and qualified real estate broker. He will probably have all of the answers for you. If he doesn't have them on tap, he can get them faster than you can in most cases.

So here we go with the thirteen National Better Business Bureau queries that we call "safe-guides."

1. *THE PROMOTER*

Who is behind the offer and the promotion? What have the experience and performance records of these persons been? KNOW WITH WHOM YOU ARE DEALING. If you don't know, consult the local Better Business Bureau or Chamber of Commerce or Realty Board in the area. Will you be dealing with a licensed real estate broker? (licensing is required in 46 states). Will you be dealing with a Realtor?

THE TRADEMARK "REALTOR" INDICATES A BROKER WHO HAS BEEN ACCEPTED INTO MEMBERSHIP IN HIS LOCAL REAL ESTATE BOARD AND THE NATIONAL ASSOCIATION OF REAL ESTATE BOARDS AND IS PLEDGED TO ITS ESTABLISHED CODE OF BUSINESS ETHICS.

2. *ADVERTISING AND DEVELOPMENTS*

If there are advertised or pictured improvements, such as paved roads, marinas, parks, beaches, golf courses, clubhouses, etc., have they been completed? Are they available for use? Or are they simply planned if the development is successful? Is there assurance that advertised improvements will be completed? Is the status of improvements indicated clearly?

Do pictures in advertising show actual portions of the development?

Are distances from facilities noted accurately, or are they described as "nearby," "at your doorstep," etc?

If prices of lots are featured in advertising, is one lot of sufficient area for a house? Are you required to buy more than one lot? (also see ZONING requirements in 13). [Authors' note: In one subdivision, lots were advertised at $495 each. When we went to inspect them we found out that a building site was *three* lots which made one plot, the minimum homesite. The minimum cost for a homesite was $1485. Quite a difference!]

3. *LOCATION*

Exactly where is the property located? Is access assured? How far from the highway? From town? From factories and industrial areas? From shopping centers or diversified neighborhood stores? From other lots and homes? From civic and community facilities such as schools, churches, hospitals, police and fire protection, garbage and rubbish removal, lighted streets, recreational facilities, etc.? How far from employment?

Is the map upon which the lot is designated a recorded (approved) plat? If so, where has it been filed?

Is the property located in an area made undesirable by odors, noises, or smoke? If beach rights and water privileges are included, are they included in the filed map and does the promoter have the right to grant such rights and privileges? [Authors' note: We know of one subdivision where the subdivider did not have legal right-of-way to the water resort and the government forced him to abandon the road he had built.]

Is it located in an area in which you will be troubled by insect pests? Would it be undesirable because of floods or subsidence? Is there any fire protection? Is there likelihood of encroachment by commercial, industrial or highway development? What are the future plans for the area? [Authors' note: Ask about climate too.]

4. *VALUE OF LAND IN AREA*

What is the current selling price of unimproved land in the immediate area of your lot? Is the price of the lots in which you are interested in keeping with the price of other available land in the immediate vicinity? Are homes in the area well maintained? Is the character of the neighborhood satisfactory? Are the surroundings desirable?

5. *STATUS OF PROPERTY*

Who owns the land? Is it free and clear? If mortgaged, insist upon knowing the exact terms from the holder. Are there any easements, liens, judgments, assessments, unpaid taxes, etc.? The title should be searched before any transaction is completed. [Author's note: In most of the western states there are excellent title companies who will search title and insure it. In the process they uncover the answers to the above questions *before* title is passed. In our opinion this service is one of the best low-cost insurance buys possible. It can save you and your heirs untold agony.]

6. *IMPROVEMENTS*

What improvements have been installed to date? Paved streets? Sidewalks? Street lights? Public utilities? Sanitary sewers? (see item 7) Storm sewers? (see item 8) Are there water mains or must individual wells be dug? How much will a well cost? Are the tax assessments and the utility rates satisfactory? (see item 11) If improvements have been installed are they paid for? If not, what portion of the burden are property holders expected to share? If they have not been installed, what plans have been made for such installation, and what are the arrangements concerning the cost? Has a bond been filed with the state or county authorities to insure completion of improvements? Who will be responsible for maintenance of improvements, utilities, etc.? Is this set forth in writing?

7. *SEWAGE*

Are there sanitary sewers or must septic tanks be put in? If septic tanks are necessary, are they authorized by local zoning statutes? Is the level of the land and type of soil suitable for septic tanks? Is local health department approval required for such tanks? Has such approval been granted?

8. *DRAINAGE*

Is the land dry or must it be drained? Is drainage feasible and possible? Have storm sewers been installed? Does the situation and location of the plot permit effective drainage after storms? Is the water table sufficiently deep so that basement and foundations are above it?

9. *SOIL*

What is the top soil analysis? Is it satisfactory for lawn and garden? Subsoil? Does the property contain fill? If so, is there a likelihood of sinkage? [Authors' note: This is particularly important in the western hill regions where much land is "created" by the cut-and-fill process. It is not unusual to hear of homes sliding off their pads or swimming pools ending up in the neighbor's yard. In an area of known natural springs or in a known earthquake-fault area this is a pertinent question.]

10. *TOPOGRAPHY*

What is the topography of the land? Will it need grading, excavating, or filling? Retaining walls? What will the costs be? Is there a rock problem?

11. *TAXES*

What is the present assessment rate? What is the assessed value of the property? Will the assessed value increase when the property is improved? When civic and community improvements have been completed? What is the increase that may be expected? Have special assessments been levied? If included in the purchase price, have they been paid? Are others in prospect?

12. *FINANCING*

If you are asked to pay so much down and so much per month over a period of years, insist upon knowing the full details of such an arrangement. If a down payment is required you may wish to discuss with your attorney the advisability of placing such payments in escrow. Are the terms of the contract subject to your ability to obtain a satisfactory mortgage from a lender of your choosing? Is there a prepayment clause? Are its provisions satisfactory?

It is not only important that the purchaser know whether he can obtain a mortgage, but whether there is an existing mortgage on the property. If so, must the buyer assume this mortage or will the seller satisfy the mortgage and discharge its lien? What are the alternatives? How much are the closing costs? Can they be included in the mortgage? If there is no mortgage what are the carrying charges, if any, on the unpaid balance, on a time payment plan? *It is advisable to retain an attorney for arranging and closing full transactions.*

13. *ZONING*

What are the local zoning restrictions and what protection do they offer? Will you have to buy more than one lot in order to comply with such zoning requirements? (see item 2) Will you have to buy more land in order to build the house you want, and still conform to local zoning regulations regarding the amount of frontage and the sidelines of the property? Are there any restrictive or protective covenants? What are their terms? Does your contemplated construction violate them?

We might add one more question: Does the area have a "progress association" or similar civic group which is determined to keep the area growing? In Southern California's Antelope Valley, two such groups have been responsible for bringing in dozens of new industrial installations which have resulted in solid growth and value increases.

Also, these progress or development associations or organizations usually will be able to tell you whether or not banks, chain stores, gas stations, savings and loan institutions, and other harbingers of progress have taken any leases in the general area or have had scouts out looking. Large oil companies often will scout an area several years in advance of its actual development, tying up good corners on long-term leases on which they are happy to pay during the vacant stage in order to have preferred position when the building starts. Any corner an oil company ties down is very apt to become an important intersection. Your realtors in the area will usually be aware of such moves and will be happy to report them to you as evidence of progress to come. Quiet incursions of conservative businesses are potent sales arguments for real estate men!

You may feel like taking a deep breath and dropping the whole idea of investing in land in favor of betting on the horses. But any dedicated horse player will do more statisti-

cal research on the bangtails in one week than you will have
to do in a month of looking if you use these safe-guides and
get your answers from qualified people.

It is all a matter of common sense, really. In this case the
National Better Business Bureau has spared us the hard work
of digging out the questions that will produce the truth about
a parcel of land . . . *if* . . . you'll take the trouble to ask
them.

If you can just remember to ask yourself the first question
. . . the primary one—"Why do I want to buy this piece of
land?"—getting the answers to the rest of the questions will
become an engrossing game, and quite likely a highly profitable one too.

We could end this chapter here but we think it's worth
adding a few more paragraphs which may help to convince
you of the soundness of following the safe-guides.

Everywhere we went, the brokers, realtors, land promoters, the buyers who had made out well, the officials of the
various county and state government groups said the same
thing. "Look before you leap! Insist upon full disclosure of
all the facts before you buy. Know the men you're giving
your money to! Know what you want. Because once you do,
there are lots of reputable men who make a business of help-
ing you find it."

Early one morning we dropped into the Grants Pass Chamber of Commerce in Oregon. We had made an appointment
the night before with Jack McMahan, manager of the
Chamber, and had asked him to have present anyone who
might be interested in contributing some common sense to a
book about western land.

It was short notice, but when we arrived at 8 A.M. County
Commissioner Donald G. McGregor and Realty Board President Fred Dayton were waiting. In an hour of informal
talk with these three fine and extremely helpful men we filled

a notebook with information about their beautiful country and a lot of on-the-button advice.

Jack McMahan summed it up as we left by saying, "Not enough buyers take advantage of the services that are at their disposal. There isn't a government official, a businessman, a banker, or a realtor in this state who wouldn't be glad to supply straight information to any serious person who is thinking of making an investment. We want the kind of people to settle here who will take the trouble to find out what this part of the country's all about. We'll give them as much help as they need!"

If the help these men gave us is any sample, then anyone with sense enough to ask the questions of them would have a hard time making a serious error in judgment in buying in the area.

The story was the same wherever we went. On the way back from Arizona we drove into Yuma about lunchtime. For some miles along the highway we'd seen real estate signs. But the most numerous seemed to be those of a man named Carl Self. On an impulse we said, "Let's go into his office and talk to him. A man who sets traps for you fifty miles out in the desert must be an enterprising broker."

We found the firm's modest office handy to a good cafe. Mr. Carl Self was not around . . . but his son, H. L. "Bud" Self, was. We stated the purpose of our visit and for the next hour, young Bud gave us a fascinating rundown of the Yuma and Wellton areas. Nowhere on our 7000 mile research trip did we meet anyone who knew more about his area. Any question, however complicated, met with an immediate answer supported by facts and figures from brochures, books, and papers published by the Arizona Development Board, by the local and state chambers of commerce, by the government farm authorities, by every possible authentic source of dependable information including the military, which has large holdings there.

There is nothing on Bud Self's card to indicate whether he is a member of the Realty Board and therefore a realtor, but certainly he is one of the best-informed brokers we have met. Later when we checked his information against that given us by Bernard Mergen, director of the Arizona Development Board in Phoenix, and by Bert Coleman, director of publicity and public relations for that board, we found everything checked out to the last decimal point. We are certain there were many other fine brokers in the area who would have done the same for us. But young Bud Self was the one we met and it was an impressive meeting.

Incidentally, one thing came up constantly when we were seeking sources of information. Almost every development board and realty board head we talked to added this piece of advice:

"The West is growing so fast that by the time we can pull the facts together and get them printed, important new material is being added. In order to be sure everything is up to the minute, go see the local newspapers. Their real estate editors and business editors are the very best sources of hour-to-hour happenings that may affect your purchase."

Of course brokers and realtors are omnivorous readers of newspapers and current magazines too. But if you are thinking about moving into an area, it seems as important to know your newspaper or newspapers and what they stand for as it is to know the city, county, and state officials whose task also is to serve the community. "A man is known by the company he keeps" might well be amended to read, "A town is known by the papers it supports and by the men it elects."

Perhaps one of the best ways to bring together the basic information of the foregoing chapters into a working example is to show how we applied our formula to the finding of our own western investment land.

First of all, as we said, we had been in the East for twenty-one years. We were coming home again and we understood (rather vaguely, we know now) that great changes had taken place not only on the Pacific coast but in most of the western states.

Once settled in Laguna Beach, California, we began thinking about our land investment program. Obviously the first thing to do was to follow the advice of our good friend Robert Preston in the song from Meredith Willson's *Music Man* that cautions, "You gotta know the territory."

Believe us, the territory had changed! First of all, the population of California had risen from about seven million in 1940, when we had left, to better than fifteen million in 1958, when we returned. In twenty years, Los Angeles itself had grown from slightly over a million to well over two and a half million.

The entire Pacific coast area had risen from fifteen million in 1950 to twenty million people by 1958.

Suburban towns, once reached by driving through miles of agricultural country, were now connected to the main body of the "megaloctopus" by solid tentacles of concrete bordered by acres of tract houses and shopping centers that had mushroomed beside the new freeways. Great new strips of suburbs reached out from city hall in every direction. Prices had skyrocketed. The land Father Cooley turned down only thirty years earlier as overpriced at $550 an acre was now in the heart of The Miracle Mile on Wilshire Blvd. . . . and it was priceless . . . being parceled out by the square foot!

Very quickly we came to the conclusion that with our modest purse there was no use looking close in any more. We had already decided that we wanted our investment to mature in about ten years. That meant inexpensive undeveloped land out on the periphery of the great strip city or megalopolis that already had reached from San Diego to Santa Barbara and was expanding by two routes along U.S. Highway 99 and along Highway 6 [now the new Antelope Valley Freeway] toward the San Joaquin Valley.

18   An "improved" road in a western recreational subdivision. The road was
put in in 1963. The area promptly got a freak rain of 14 inches in three days.
The result was many thousands of dollars worth of damage. Who will repair
it? The subdivider murmurred vaguely about "the county." The county officials
were not so vague. They said flatly, "We have not taken over those streets yet.
The repairs are up to the subdivider!" In the end, costly repairs may be up to
the various people who purchased in the tract. How to protect yourself? *See
"Thirteen Lucky Questions," Chapter Eight.*

19　California's Antelope Valley Freeway with grading about completed. Notice progress on terraced cuts near center of picture. The superhighway will put the valley and its huge aero-space center, Edwards Air Force Base, within easy commuting distance of metropolitan Los Angeles and within minutes of the San Fernando Valley.　(*Photo by State of California, Department of Public Works, Division of Highways*)

20　Three years later, September 1966, next to last link of Antelope Valley Freeway is dedicated just west of the City of Palmdale. No longer a "land promoter's pipe dream," this super-freeway brings metropolitan Los Angeles within minutes of a vast new agricultural and industrial empire. Dozens of new suburban subdivisions are springing up along the new freeway, building yet another strip city in Southern California.　(*Photo by State of California, Department of Public Works, Division of Highways*)

21   The town of Palmdale, California, on Highway 6 looking northeast, showing Southern Pacific main line (foreground) to the San Joaquin Valley and the San Francisco area. In the distance (arrow) is U.S.A.F. Plant 42. The new Antelope Valley Freeway will parallel Highway 6 (shown) and the railroad several miles to the west (left).   *(Photo by Bill Penn, Antelope Valley Progress Association)*

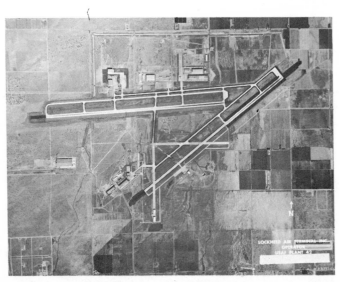

22   U.S. Air Force Plant 42 at Palmdale, California, showing the two 10,000 foot runways able to accommodate controversial new Super-Sonic Transport. Colonel Clifford L. Rawson, Palmdale's Director of Economic Development, advised us that Mayor Larry Chimbole's three-year negotiations for joint military-commercial usage of this ultra-modern airport may soon result in new commercial terminal, ramp, concourse, and maintenance facilities. Enjoying 350 days of flying weather per year, this facility could become the principal SST International Terminal for Southern California.   *(Photo by Antelope Valley Progress Association)*

23   Eight miles north of Palmdale on Highway 6 is Lancaster, California, heart of the Emerald Triangle Area of the Antelope Valley. The space-age industries at nearby Edwards Air Force Base (just beyond upper right-hand corner of photo) and "people pressure" from the Los Angeles megalopolis have created a phenomenal growth in this area. The town's main street, Lancaster Ave., (arrow) has spread ten blocks in the past three years. The new Antelope Valley Freeway to Rosamond and the industrial center of Mohave will cut through upper left-hand corner of photo. This entire town area was once almost solidly planted in alfalfa.   (*Photo by Antelope Valley Progress Association*)

24   A perfect example of "people pressure" at work. This new Sears Roebuck super-store in Lancaster now occupies the alfalfa field in the lower left hand corner of Plate 23 at the top of this page! In 1950 this land averaged $500 an acre. Ten years later it went for ten times that amount.   (*Hart Printers, Lancaster*)

25   The very heart of West Hellangone! Our weary "Bird" parked in the middle of a 2½-acre plot "suitable for farming with all utilities available."

26   It helps to keep a sense of humor. (The co-author had a struggle with hers when she saw this portrait!) The wind was 30 knots, the thermometer stood at 30 degrees. The intersection of the two main thoroughfares on which "this beautiful corner lot" is located may be dimly visible in the foreground to those with active imaginations.

27   The ultramodern Lake Mead Marina, a floating marina and restaurant at Boulder Beach, Nevada. These are the resorts that land developers, usually miles away on dirt roads, refer to as being "adjacent to" or "within easy driving distance of" their remote desert "vacation paradises." Some of them are. (*Photo by National Park Service, Boulder City, Nevada*)

28   Aerial photo of Lake Mohave resort at Katherine, Arizona. Seen here are the camp grounds, National Park Service residences, trailer village, motel, picnic shelters, marina, and swimming beach. People drive hundreds of desert miles to enjoy these public parks.

29   Air shot of Hollywood (in foreground) and the great San Fernando Valley around 1930, then just beginning its suburban development as the budding megalopolis of Los Angeles embraces Hollywood and Beverly Hills and moves outward over the new Cahuenga Pass road, seen snaking across the barrier hills to Lankershim (now North Hollywood) just to right of center of the photo. The arrow indicates the approximate site of the great new shopping center shown in accompanying photo.   (*Photo from Title Insurance and Trust Company, Los Angeles, Collection of Historical Photographs*)

30   The Ventura Freeway winds its way southwestward through Sherman Oaks and Van Nuys and over the hills to Hollywood via Cahuenga Pass. On this amazing high-speed road motorists may now go from Ventura, California, to San Diego without a stop.   (*Photo by California State Division of Highways*)

31 Looking toward Hollywood from Wilshire Boulevard (in foreground) in 1922. The dirt road wandering through the oil rigs to the right is Highland Ave. On the left is La Brea Ave. The then sparsely settled San Fernando Valley lies just beyond the Hollywood hills. Wilshire Boulevard was a two-lane "paved" street. (*Photo by Title Insurance and Trust Company, Los Angeles, Collection of Historical Photographs*)

32 1936 — Fourteen Years Later! The jack rabbits, the farms, and the oil fields have given way to blocks of residences, to apartment buildings, to stores, theaters, schools. The four vacant blocks along Wilshire Boulevard (lower right hand) are now built solid with towering steel and glass office buildings. Today a front foot of this property sells for more than a standard lot sold for in the same area just fourteen years earlier. (*Photo by Title Insurance and Trust Company, Los Angeles, Collection of Historical Photographs*)

So, practicing what we preach, we began a series of exploration trips. Each weekend we would head out in a different direction until finally we had explored the entire Southern California region for two hundred miles around Los Angeles.

We saw many exciting areas. But when we started talking to the realtors, the brokers, the businessmen, the people who had bought earlier and had held, we soon realized that for our purpose most of the acreage was far too expensive. Without being arbitrary about it we had set a figure of $600 an acre as the top price we would pay for our initial investment. We wanted land that would show reasonable promise of increasing in *net* value by at least 10 per cent per year for ten years.

We loved the beautiful avocado and citrus land in the "Leo Carrillo country" around Vista and Fallbrook just inland from the coastline at Oceanside. We "goofed" here perhaps, primarily because we were slow in our research and did not listen to an old friend Roy Bargy, who had been our musical director on the "Lanny Ross Show" on CBS Radio in the early 1940s and who, though still musical director for "The Jimmy Durante Show," has become a respected broker in Vista.

Roy advised us to buy some acreage at just under $1000 an acre in 1958. But we waited too long. It went for $1500 an acre in less than a year. We were wrong—according to hindsight. But on the other hand perhaps we were not because we feel that the best thing in the long run is to stick to your economic blueprint even though occasionally you may sacrifice flexibility. It is a sticky point, really—one upon which a number of experts have differing views. A reassuring number of them concur with ours.

The beautiful Anza Valley was another area where we might have bought. The prices were right for us then and there were other good signs: new roads planned, ample

water, a splendid mountain resort area within a few minutes' drive. But we continued to look. We wanted, if possible, to locate the next area in Southern California most
likely to feel the full brunt of people pressure because it lay
in the path of the major flow of strip-city development. Several times we were tempted to move; but each time when we
appraised our research and equated it with the information
received from bankers, brokers, and newspaper editors in
the area, we felt the need to look further.

Although we had gone as far north as the Lancaster–Palmdale area in the Antelope Valley, we had been thrown off a
bit by a persistent and shortsighted rumor that terminating
defense contracts at the huge U.S. Air Force Plant 42 in
Palmdale had brought about a local recession there. Certainly there were a number of vacant tract houses, despite
the fact that the tremendous nearby space complex that is
Edwards Air Force Base was constantly expanding and playing a more vital role in development of the X-15. We held off.

Several times we came close to decisions in other areas.
Time has proved that we would have chosen well in almost
any of the other areas that interested us. But just before we
reached a final decision we stopped in at the Antelope Valley
Progress Association offices in Lancaster and asked for the
latest literature. In the kit was a map we hadn't seen. It
showed a proposed new, high-speed road to be known as the
Antelope Valley Freeway. Also the map showed several other
proposed freeways cutting across the area we would later
come to call the "Emerald Triangle," whose boundaries run
roughly from Gorman on Highway 99 northeastward to California City, then southwestward to Valyermo and north-
westward again to Gorman.

A talk with the manager of the Lancaster branch of the
Bank of America and his opposite number, at the Security
First National Bank in the same city, seemed to indicate a

significant amount of unconfirmed rumor concerning not one but three freeways in the planning stage.

Our next stop was at the California State Department of Public Works Building in downtown Los Angeles. There, in the offices of the Division of Highways, we were given the "straight scoop" on the Antelope Valley Freeway, on the probability of Highway 138 being made into a freeway, and on the plans for converting Highway 466 into a freeway from Bakersfield to Barstow and perhaps on beyond to Las Vegas.

This is what we were looking for! These were the new *major arteries* along which *people pressure* could most easily and logically be expected to exert its full force if the proposed plans became reality.

A few more weeks of watching newspapers and magazines —of talking to anyone who might know something—and then we were ready to make our move. We knew now it would be in the Antelope Valley.

We had been talking with a number of brokers during the "looking" stage. One of those brokers seemed best geared to our way of buying so we went back and talked things over.

The following week this thorough-going land pro had a handful of listings for us to run down. Very patiently he drove us all over that incredible valley. It is a valley of contrasts—rich gold mines overlooking alfalfa fields that produce six crops a season; cotton fields next to raw desert that awaits only the plow and the plentiful water to burgeon with bumper crops of almost anything a farmer wants to plant.

All told there are 25,000 square miles in its 69+ townships and nearly 60 per cent of its area is either planned and zoned or in the planning process. Two major railroads serve the valley, the Southern Pacific and the Santa Fe. Historically, both have been major factors in the growth of the West.

In addition to the three contemplated freeways (all of

them now under construction or budgeted—the final sixteen-mile link in the Antelope Valley Freeway connecting with Los Angeles will be open by the time this book is published) there is a network of fine, surfaced roads connecting each part of the valley. Existing water supplies are ample for a population growth totalling a million persons—a census expected considerably *before* the 1980 "guesstimate."

The climate is ideal: high desert, generally mild, absolutely smog-free (a must for us), sunshine for over 300 days of the year, close to ten inches of annual rainfall, and humidity that seldom exceeds a comfortable 40 per cent even in winter.

For the next two weeks we drove our car, or drove with the broker, looking at acreage. During these trips and the overnight stays at one of the scores of fine motels, hotels, and other tourist facilities in the valley, we studied more of the fact sheets given us by Clifford Rawson, executive director of the Antelope Valley Progress Association.

True to predictions, things were changing so fast that most of the material had to be updated from week to week by phone calls to the association office.

Finally, about a month after our own personal "discovery" of the Antelope Valley, we chose the land that was destined to become the first of many purchases. Using profit from the sale of investment land in the East, we purchased an 80-acre piece of beautiful level land high on the alluvial shelf of the Tehachapi Mountains just north of historic Willow Springs on the Kern County side of the valley.

In the year of our Declaration of Independence, 1776, Father Francisco Gracés had stopped at the springs after leaving the Mission San Gabriel. He became the second white man to cross the Tehachapi Mountains into the great south central valley of the San Joaquin.

During the Civil War era, the Havilah Stage Line ran Concord coaches drawn by six horses through these rugged mountains, roughly following the trail John C. Frémont had pioneered some twenty years earlier in 1844. It is not difficult to imagine our feelings today as we travel that historic Willow Springs Road after having read General Frémont's personal account of the trip in his *Narratives of Exploration and Adventure* written slightly over one hundred years ago. A knowledge of the history of the area in which you buy will add immeasurably to its value—perhaps not in dollars and cents but in other ways equally important. Soon, with the completion of Highway 466 as a major freeway connecting with the new Antelope Valley Freeway, autos and trucks will traverse historic Tehachapi Pass in a matter of minutes. It took Frémont nearly three days!

The thirteen "safe-guides" of the National Better Business Bureau were applied before the purchase, of course. On no count did we have to make a major concession. There was no electric power right at the property but that did not matter to us since it was ten-year hold land.

Three water wells on three sides of us gave reasonable promise that our land would have ample water, too, if needed. There was telephone service only 200 yards from the property line. But everything else was right on the button, including the price (below our top) and the taxes.

That original 80 acres has grown to quite a few hundred acres in the same area . . . all of it ten-year hold land. We get a wonderful feeling now as we drive out to our growing valley and behold the miracles happening all around us. When we first started going out to visit our property we could stand on its high tableland at sundown and watch the most breath-taking full-color, wide-screen sunsets imaginable. Then, as darkness fell, we'd see below us and off to the southwest the lights of Lancaster, Palmdale, and Quartz Hill beginning to wink on. In 1959 there were three isolated light clusters about eight miles apart. Between them and us the other lights were few and widely scattered.

Now, when darkness falls and the stars seem to settle down on our shoulders like a celestial mantle, we watch those earthbound lights blink on. But no longer are the three towns isolated islands of light; now they blend into one long, luminous strip between Highway 14 and Sixtieth St. West, an area presently bisected by the final link of the freeway now under construction. More than that, the once scattered lights in the valley are beginning to fill in. Little by little they are "gaining on us."

Landvalues in the Antelope Valley's Emerald Triangle area have risen spectacularly within the past year on the strength of the new freeway and upon the passage of California's 1.75 billion-dollar Feather River Water Project, which will bring 120,000 acre feet of mountain water into the area in addition to the 40,000 acre feet of artesian water now available. We didn't count the possibility of the Feather River Project in our considerations in 1958–59 because then it, too, was just a "long-range plan" that the voters might reject—"if it ever got on the ballot!"

The point is that we have minimized the gamble in every single undeveloped land investment we have made since we learned—sometimes the hard way—how to go about locating the likely places to buy.

We have no hesitancy or superstition at all in saying that we have never lost money on a piece of land—nor do we ever expect to—as long as we follow the basic principles outlined in the foregoing chapters and apply them as we have demonstrated in these last few paragraphs.

The main point is—*you can do it too*—with just as much certainty—*if* you will take the time and the very little trouble to go a-lookin'!

9

THE ANATOMY OF A MURDEROUS INVESTMENT

Shortly after Milton G. Gordon took office as California Real Estate Commissioner we met with him in the office of Assistant Commissioner Gerald E. Harrington, head of the Southern California Division.

Commissioner Gordon and his staff were deeply involved in new legislation intended to make California's already efficient real estate laws still more effective in protecting the buyer.

When we told the commissioner that as Californians we were proud of our state's laws—that other states considered them among the best in the country because of California's record of not having been the home ground of highly questionable subdivision developments such as some of those we had seen, he said, "This is not just a chance happening. As California's population has grown rapidly to top the nation, there has been a great deal of subdividing, but it has been under local and state regulation, the latter based on the "full disclosure" principle.

"A public report prepared by the Real Estate Commissioner for prospective purchasers gives a factual account of the land, state of title, improvements, utilities, financing, sales plan, etc. But the legislature and the Governor in 1963 decided that the public was entitled to more protection than the 'full disclosure' principle provides. The law has been changed to give the Real Estate Commissioner the power to withhold a public report on a proposed California subdivision under certain circumstances. For example, if the subdivider appears unable to deliver title or the interest contracted for, or if he cannot demonstrate satisfactorily that adequate financial arrangements have been made for off-site improvements, or for community, recreational or other facilities included in the offering, or if he fails to show that the parcels can be used for the purpose for which they are offered, the report will not be issued.

"To protect the California public from the blandishments of promoters who would through the mails or by other means entice them into 'investing' in out-of-state land of dubious value and no present utility, another law has gone on the California books this year. Under its terms the Real Estate Commissioner makes an examination of out-of-state subdivisions to determine if the offering would be fair, just and equitable. If the offering does not meet these standards, the Real Estate Commissioner can refuse to permit the properties to be sold in the State of California.

"As a result," concluded Commissioner Gordon, "California has much stronger subdivision regulations than ever before and it is encouraging to note that other states are moving in the same direction to protect their citizens from unscrupulous land promoters."

New Mexico, Arizona, Nevada, and Oregon have taken steps to protect buyers and some of the provisions have been

modeled on California's rigid requirements; Florida is struggling to come up with a more effective law. But alas, in some
states apathy still allows the Paradise Peddlers to operate
unhampered by effective restrictions.

Because the slippery promoter and con man will always be
with us in one endeavor or another, the other western states
are re-examining their present real estate laws in the certain
knowledge that as states get tougher to operate in the
crooked promoter will seek cheap raw land in easier states
that have not yet mended their subdivision fences.

It seems reasonable, however, that any state official would
concede that one of the best early defenses against the unscrupulous land operator is plain old common sense on the
part of the buyer.

Actually it is not really too difficult to spot the unethical
land promoter who would hold you up for thousands of dollars with nothing more than a few plausible lies and a loaded
fountain pen. They all use approximately the same tactics.
And the result to the victim is nearly always the same. We
think this was summed up very succinctly on a homemade
sign we saw on a parcel of sand and sagebrush in one of the
western desert subdivisions now under state and federal investigation. The sign read, simply:

DON'T BORROW TROUBLE. OWN IT OUTRIGHT!

Owner will sell this gorgeous
corner of paradise for $100 cash.

There was also a P.O. box address . . . in an eastern city.
We wrote to the man to get his story but so far we've had
no reply. Undoubtedly he suspects more shenanigans. If this
book should fall into his hands perhaps he will wish he had
replied. We would have given him a chance to blow his
stack and tell his story. On the other hand perhaps he would

not have cared to confess publicly that he fell for the deliberate deceptions, the half-truths, the illusions, and the allusions employed by the unscrupulous land salesman.

Like any crook, the land shark has a lot of modern tools at his disposal. But alert legislators throughout the country are making sure these tools are not improperly used. Already most of the states are alert to the problem, as we've said, and are sharpening up legislation to protect the unwary buyer. But newspapers, magazines, radio, and television cannot possibly screen all of the firms who use their services to sell products to the public. Generally the advertising contracts are placed through advertising agencies. Some of them are "house agencies" owned or controlled by the advertiser himself . . . set up as separate corporations.

Often then, seemingly harmless advertising finds its way to the public because the advertiser's credit is okay and the ads do not violate the media's own code of ethics.

The competition for advertising dollars is among the roughest in business. Because it is, perhaps some papers, magazines, radio and television men don't have time to check as thoroughly as they might like to. After all, they have access to the Better Business bureaus and other agencies too. A man leaves a business record just as surely as he leaves a criminal record. In the cases of disreputable land men, it is not uncommon to find extremely questionable records, sometimes of an outright criminal nature. Often they have operated in many easy-money swindles. It is the tragic truth that a very few of these operators can "tar with the same brush" a lot of completely ethical men operating in the same businesses.

It is worth reminding you of that so that you won't be tempted to dismiss all land promoters as questionable operators. The unwary buyer who has been burned in one bad land deal is like the drunk with the Limburger cheese under his nose: he's convinced the whole world stinks. To that we

might moralize that if he'd kept his head and not fallen for a
something-for-nothing pitch he'd have come out of the deal
with his nose a lot cleaner!

Some of the buyers have a sense of humor about their own
private desert paradises in "the heart of West Hellangone."
In the middle of one huge, sun-baked, totally unimproved
subdivision on which we were later told it would be impossible for the seller to deliver clear title, we found a weath-
ered piece of paper wrapped around an old mesquite stump.
On it, in pencil, had been crudely printed this typical example of western hospitality:

YOU ARE WELCOME TO CAMP ON OUR LAND
ABSOLUTELY FREE FROM JUNE THROUGH OCTOBER.
WE HAVE GONE TO HELL TO COOL OFF!

But again let us point out that, within seeing distance of
both these signs, we talked to people who were living on
their parcels of land twelve months a year and were happy
about it.

For the most part we agree with a recent editorial in the
Mojave County Miner in Kingman, Arizona. In the interest
of simple justice, it is worth reproducing here. It is headed,
"It's Not too Late to Act." It says:

In the last year a great deal has been written about Mojave County's land promotion and speculation deals. Most
of what has captured the attention of the national magazines and newspapers has not been complimentary of what
has been done here.

Those of us who live here and love our county have been
disturbed at the tone of some of the articles.

We haven't been disturbed at the exposing of the promotions which have been either downright illegal or in bad taste.

But we have been disturbed at the fact that most of the reporters who have visited the area have simply refused to even acknowledge the fact that we have some very wholesome developments here too.

We have had these men visit our office and go through our files. We have discussed the situation candidly and have told them that while there have been several deals that have drawn the fire of federal and state officials, that many of our developments have been good.

The Colorado Riviera is a showplace. Lake Mojave Ranchos has attracted a number of people who appear to us to be most content with their situation. Elmer Butler's New Kingman Estates is rapidly filling up with people who seem to be well satisfied that they bought the property.

Over the course of a year, many people visit the offices of this newspaper. Last summer a large number of these visitors were from the east. They had bought a desert lot and wanted to see it.

Without exception every person who came into this office expressed satisfaction with their purchase. We would feel a lot better about some of these articles if the reporters would talk to some of the pioneer people who bought this land—and moved on to it.

Some have to haul water—but they don't seem to mind. Some are without utilities—but they don't seem to mind.

The point is that—(the magazines and the newspapers were listed here)—and all the other periodicals which have taken roundhouse swings at Mojave County fail to recognize that some people like this country so well they'd live here if they had to haul water fifty miles.

Not all our developments are plush. But a few of them have been developed in bad taste. We have been handed a pretty dirty rap by some of these writers who came here convinced it was all bad before they ever saw it.

We admit that in the beginning we took a dim view of the developments. But we've seen some of the real good that can be done and have changed our mind. We see nothing wrong with selling of desert acreage if it is advertised fairly and truthfully.

If it is not—the people guilty of fraud should go to jail.

But what some people fail to recognize is that there are people and quite a few of them at that, who would rather live on a five acre tract in the middle of the desert without utilities and having to haul water, than to live in any part of Detroit, Los Angeles or Brooklyn.

If memory of history serves us correctly, some Eastern newspapers thought the Gadsden Purchase was a bad deal too.[1]

[1] An area of 45,535 sq. miles now comprising Southern New Mexico and Southern Arizona south of the Gila River. It was purchased by the United States from Mexico in 1854 for $10,-000,000, in order to stabilize our border, insure possession of the Mesilla Valley along the Rio Grande and secure the most practical route for a southern transcontinental railroad. It was negotiated by James Gadsden. Though we do not wish to whitewash by inference any of the unscrupulous promoters who deserve to be prosecuted, it is interesting that James Gadsden, like his contemporary pioneer General John C. Frémont, was reprimanded for exceeding his authority. As it turned out, a little more than a hundred years ago Gadsden purchased that land for us for about $2.90 an acre—or less than the assessed value of most third class range land today . . . and the purchase contained barren land destined to become some of the

These people simply cannot believe that, in this day of trips to the moon and atom bombs, there are still pioneers-at-heart who have been hemmed-in in big city apartments all their lives, never owning a thing, who are tickled pink to own something and dream of the future, even if it's only five acres in the middle of the desert in Mojave County.

We have been handed some bad publicity.

But we'll live through it—and come back stronger than ever before. This is great country and it will get greater.

But to help it become greater, we will need to plan even more solidly for the future.

This newspaper has suggested on numerous occasions that we need a county-wide zoning and planning ordinance more than any other single thing. Other Arizona counties have these ordinances and they serve a very worthwhile purpose. Just recently Undersecretary of Interior Graham Hollister advised us of the need for zoning and planning in the lower Colorado River development area.

Had Mojave County set up a system of zoning a few years ago when it was originally planned to do so, this bad publicity could have been avoided. It would have been avoided because regulations governing subdivisions would have already been in effect.

It is not too late to rectify this situation.

The Mojave County Board of Supervisors should proceed immediately to establish a commission to start studying this proposition. It has been done with great success

most valuable in the United States. As these far sighted (and ofttimes selfish gents) would tell you if they could, "It's tough to be a pioneer!"

elsewhere and could be a great measure of protection for Mojave County.

It is better to take some positive action to protect our present and future residents than to just sit back and cry about the bad publicity we are getting now.

In the authors' opinion this editorial, in substance, might well be the appeal of every county in every western state where such zoning regulations are sorely needed . . . and that would be in just about every county where subdivided raw land is sold. Even in counties where such regulations exist, the restrictions vary widely. They tend to be more stringent in those counties in which large concentrations of population have become metropolises and are now in the process of becoming megalopolises.

In a letter from Kenneth R. Blackman, planning consultant for the Klamath Community Planning Office in Klamath Falls, Oregon, the problem was expressed still again. In answer to our query about one subdivision of so-called "recreational land" advertised in leading California papers he said:

"This is actually one of the 'better' developments of a recreational nature which we have in Klamath County. It complies with the somewhat meager restrictions of our County subdivision ordinance, which is more than can be said for many of the developments within the county which have been nationally advertised."

One is naturally led to ask, "Why, if you have a county subdivision ordinance and you have evidence that it is being violated, don't you invoke the law and stop these operators?"

But we soon found out the answer to that one. "Most counties have neither the personnel nor the budget to investigate, bring charges and prosecute the alleged violators," said one Oregon county official.

As another county official put it, "If we lost a counter-damage suit against these multimillion dollar swindlers, we'd bankrupt our county treasury! The job is too big for us now. It's a job for the state . . . but we've got to have the laws at that level first." Sometimes those laws are slow getting through the complex political mill.

The simple truth seems to be that, despite all predictions, the population explosion in the United States has come upon us so suddenly that we have just not been able to isolate its many problems, estimate the many areas where abuses could crop up, and legislate the safeguards needed to cope with them.

First to feel the pain of injury is government at the community and county level. And these bodies are the least able to cope with a national abuse of their local areas. It is their cries however that have alerted the state governments and sent legislatures into session to enact laws to bring relief, justice, and future protection.

And in all fairness we should point out too that despite their sometimes "slanted" features on western land developments or promotions it has been the free press, heeding the anguished cry of the local government and echoing it in its pages, that has brought the national scope of the problem to the attention of the Attorney General in Washington.

Most of the advertising that has come under the scrutiny of the authorities is a semanticist's nightmare. Shadings of meanings of the same words are the tenuous evidence upon which multimillion dollar lawsuits have been won or lost. It is almost impossible to determine the *real* intent behind the use of such harmless phrases as "only minutes away from . . ."; "adjacent to . . ."; "livable the year around . . ."; "all utilities available now . . ."; "just one of the many improvements planned for this growing community . . ."; "high, dry, invigorating desert-mountain climate . . ."; "already staked out, waiting for you!"

We could fill pages with such advertising copy. Obviously it is intended to sell property . . . to make it look attractive. And, the subdivider can rationalize every word of it. But let's just look at how we, prospective customers, would have interpreted it in the light of the "absolute facts" with which we would have to live:

"Only minutes away from . . ." When does an attraction like Salton Sea, Lake Mojave, Lake Mead, Lake Tahoe, Lake Arrowhead, Klamath Lake, or the Rio Grande River stop being "minutes away" and start being "miles away"? The law has not yet defined that. Neither have the semantic constructionists. But common sense has, so far as we're concerned. The intent must obviously be to make an attractive point seem closer than it is. "Minutes away" could be misleading. We feel a more direct statement would have been better for sales. Something like this perhaps: "By state highway, Lake So-and-So Resort is 35 miles distant. If you travel at the allowable speed limit, as most folks do in this open country, you can be there in 35 minutes . . . less time than it usually takes to get home through traffic."

Most fair-minded folks would call that a reasonable statement and have more faith in the promoter for laying it on the line.

A little later we're going to give you some examples of that kind of "on the line" advertising and tell you what it appears to have done for one successful Phoenix land promoter who has adopted this "head-on approach" to his sales.

Now let's look at "adjacent to . . ." The dictionary says the word means, "lying near, close or contiguous, adjoining, neighboring. . . ."

One subdivision advertised itself as "adjacent to Lake So-and-So" when by actual driving distance it was over 50 miles on the only improved road, plus another 18 miles on a rough-graded "ranch road." By their definition Moscow, Russia, is adjacent to Moscow, Idaho!

"Livable the year around . . ." is another semantic razzle-dazzle. Any place is livable the "year around" what with air conditioning, refrigeration, peripheral heating, special clothing, water purification, electrical generation, gas illumination, preventive medication, or constant abnegation! If we seem to use Arizona's really fabulous artificial lake resort area as a frequent example it is because so much of the controversy centers there. It is a prime target for the best of the selling techniques, and also for a few examples of the worst, as fair-minded Arizonans are quick to admit.

At Temple Bar Landing on Lake Mead, we dropped into the waterfront coffee shop and found a lot of the "new natives" gathered there to opine about the cold wave that had sent temperatures below freezing all over the nation.

If we had known then that we were going to quote the gentleman with whom we struck up the usual conversation about "unusual" weather we would have made it a point to get his name. But we didn't. We think, however, that he won't mind, and we know that his point of view is typical of the loyalty of those folks who live in small houses and trailers in the areas "only minutes away" from the lake.

"Well yes," he admitted, somewhat begrudgingly, "it does get a little warm here in the summer . . . even right here on the water. But you take last summer, for instance—now it wasn't bad at all. I don't believe they was hardly more'n two weeks or so when it got up over 115."

To the uninitiated those are pretty "hairy" words. But the truth is we have seen close to 100 degrees for days on end in New York City . . . with the humidity (which causes the real suffering) standing in the 80 to 90 per cent range all of the time.

And last summer in Washington State's beautiful mountain-bound Methow and Okanogan valleys the temperature often stood well over 100 degrees. But like the days at Lake Mead, the humidity was almost nonexistent and a person stayed dry and quite comfortable . . . very comfortable in the air-cooled houses and public buildings. We don't recommend going out hatless to do hard physical labor at midday in any of our western valleys during the summer months. But we do state, categorically, that a summer thermometer standing at 100 degrees is nothing to get in a sweat about . . . particularly out west with all of the inexpensive air cooling available. In the low-humidity area we often want to put more moisture back into the air with evaporation coolers to increase the comfort factor. What a contrast to the eastern states where over half of the electrical energy used by an air conditioner is spent in wringing the humidity *out* of the air!

"All utilities available now . . ." is another one to look out for. Sure they are, in some cases, if you don't mind paying several thousand dollars to bring electricity and water in to your place from the present terminal location "adjacent to our community." Remember Al Cook, our postman? He told us electricity and water were available six miles from his rancho. In some instances, it could cost a family from four to ten times their purchase price to bring the pipes and poles to the property. Gas is no problem because of the wide availability of inexpensive LP bottled fuel. Most of the pioneer settlers of today have it, "buffalo chips" being in short supply these days.

In Al's case the utilities are quite near compared to some of the places we saw.* One development in the Pacific Northwest advertised electricity was available to the property. When we checked the "public report" required by the California Division of Real Estate before any subdivider may sell within our state boundaries, we read:

ELECTRICITY: Electric service is not installed to this tract. Pacific Power & Light Co. will serve this area. Present facilities are at a distance of one to four miles from

* "People pressure" at work in Dolan Springs.

lots in this tract. Costs of approximately $1.00 per foot plus transformer service and meter installation would depend upon the number of customers and other factors including the electrical load required.

It doesn't take a computer to figure that at $1.00 a foot, it would take $5280, plus transformer service and meter installation, to bring the power into the lots only a mile from the present service terminal. If the lots were four miles away, it would come to a *lot* of money indeed!

We know for instance that the moon is "available now," too, but the cost of "bringing" the blessings of civilization to it at present give pause even to the most dedicated billion dollar "budgeteers" in Washington. The word "available" is susceptible of some of the most latitudinarian interpretation. Beware of it!

". . . just one of the many improvements planned for this growing community." Now here is one where the subdivider's heart of gold may turn stone cold when he is confronted with having made a promise to "see through" these projects that made the deal seem so attractive in the ads.

We must admit, however, that in most of the major promotions we visited the promoters had been wise enough to spend much of their "front money" on actually putting in club houses, golf courses, swimming pools, riding stables, and the like. They understand that the actual picture of the facilities completed or under construction are worth ten thousand printed words of promises and worth hundreds of thousands of dollars in land contracts. Most of the knowledgeable men expect to lay out money for at least one such facility before they get any substantial sales return. It's frosting on the cake . . . or, in the case of the unethical operator who may start but not complete the facilities, the bait in the trap. You'd better make sure whether the attractions in the subdivision are frosting or bait. Better Business Bureaus in the area can answer that for you . . . if the subdivider won't.

Another point to remember too: The price you are asked to pay for your rancho, or plot, or lot, or whatever, may be based upon the estimated worth of the land *after* such improvements are a fact. If you are going to have a prayer of a chance of getting your money's worth now and a profit later, you'd better make certain you are going to get what you pay for, at least within a reasonable period of time. Laws requiring promoters to post a performance bond would insure this, according to many officials.

"High, dry, healthful desert-mountain climate . . ." is a peachy-dandy job of weasel-wording too. We've talked about climate in a previous paragraph, but since weather is an inexhaustible topic everywhere let's give it one more whirl. "A desert-mountain climate" by any sensible definition simply doesn't exist in any one place at any one time. It's geographically impossible and it seems likely that the hyphenated hoax was devised to brainwash a buyer with a subjective image of "mountain means high and high means cool."

High desert is generally about ten degrees cooler in summer and ten degrees colder in winter than low desert.

Many of the western subdivisions are in high desert country, where elevations range from 2000 to 6000 feet. The developments in and around Palm Springs, the Salton Sea and the Coachella and Imperial valleys, and along the lower Colorado River are low desert. In the case of the Salton Sea area much of its vicinity, like the sea itself, lies several hundreds of feet *below* sea level. In the winter it is quite warm, generally. In the summer it is blazing hot, invariably! But again, modern technology has made all of these places highly livable—*if* you prepare your home to cope with Mother Nature's whims.

If we were to go into detail about air conditioning and insulation, and all the rest, this book would quite possibly be longer than the transcripts of the mail-fraud suits that seem to be in the offing against unscrupulous land dividers. Ask the local air-conditioning man about your needs in any area you might be considering. But remember, air conditioners run on electricity. If the "juice" is still $5280 or more away from your property, better figure on a good gasoline generator as part of your basic expense to make your desert hideaway livable.

One last thing about desert climate or mountain climate or any imagined combination of same: It can get good and hot during the day at altitudes of 10,000 feet as any Sierra Club hiker or dedicated trout fisherman knows. But above 3000 feet, it generally cools down at night. At our high desert place at Willow Springs in the Antelope Valley, we have often resorted to a light blanket at night as do most of the people who live or weekend in the area. The same may not be said for an "unconditioned" house in the low desert in the summer although often it is quite pleasant in the midsummer evenings.

In any case we are inclined to think that too much fuss is made about climate in the West. We say again, it's both good and bad; but today you can generally live with it by pushing the right button.

As these revisions are being made the 89th Congress is considering a brace of bills intended to place more restraints on interstate land sales.

At hearings before a subcommittee of the Senate Committee on Banking and Currency a number of persons interested in various aspects of land development, sales and investment were invited to offer both written and oral testimony. We were included in this invitation and were asked to make some observations for the record based upon our own investigations of subdivided land throughout the entire country.

After reading the proposed legislation carefully, and wrestling with our consciences, we replied in a letter addressed to Senator Harrison A. Williams, Jr. and in due time received an acknowledgment from the senator together with a printed copy of the proceedings.

In effect the new legislation would place interstate land sales under the jurisdiction of the Securities Exchange Commission whose authority would be spelled out in an interstate land sales full disclosure act.

While there is little doubt that many abuses exist and must be corrected, it is a fact that most of the states in which the abuses exist have taken, or are in the process of taking, definite and effective steps to curb the unethical operator.

In view of this fact, and because of the ever-increasing influence of the Federal Government on our economy, much of which has been made necessary by our population explosion, we could not in good conscience endorse a law that seemed to us to penalize the ethical operator by making the transaction of business even more difficult.

We suggested that perhaps congress could consider some interim legislation to be administered by the SEC that would provide reasonable protection to the purchaser of subdivided land where such protection was not already provided under existing state law.

Our idea, based on California's new, stringent, but essentially fair subdivision law, would have imposed the federal law on such sales until the state law had been revised up to or beyond the federal standard.

We were not alone in opposing a blanket federal law that would have forced legitimate land developers to comply with both federal and state laws. The physical problems of processing subdivisions through two or more such agencies would have added enormously to the cost of the finally approved land and, in most cases, would not have resulted in substantially increased protection, in the view of most ethical land men.

However, the testimony, both written and oral, before the subcommittee hearings on Senate Bill 2672 (subsequently set aside) was illuminating. No one could have read it without being painfully aware of the myriad abuses perpetrated by get-rich-quick land dealers, many of whom decided to take a flyer on "a good thing" without any previous experience. In the main, the developers who gave the whole industry a black eye were these opportunists. Some of them were downright crooks who later were judged, found guilty and penalized. But because of the widespread publicity attending their exposure many an honest developer got "tarred with the same brush."

As has been demonstrated, unscrupulous men can find loopholes in the most stringent laws. One such was found recently in California's new law and was hastily plugged up with additional legislation. So, we might paraphrase a well-known saying (which is in itself a paraphrase) by reminding prospective buyers that "eternal vigilance is the price of peace of mind" in any aspect of land dealing.

Elsewhere in this book we note that, "no law can protect a dedicated damned fool from himself." That simply means that no law or combination of laws, be they federal, state, county, or township, can do more than *half the job* of insuring a fair transaction. Unfortunately it is the sellers who are organized into entities, not the buyers. Therefore they become bearers of the burden of legal responsibility while the buyer cannot even be forced to read the laws passed for his protection.

Ethical dealers know this and consider a major part of their obligation *the protection of their customers*. Behind every successful land development you will find this philosophy. The moral is self-evident.

Before we wind up this chapter, there are a couple of more

33   Dramatic evidence of the growth of the sprawling San Francisco megaloctopus. Portions of San Francisco County (upper left hand) and San Mateo
County (lower right half) are shown here. The two golf courses were "out in
the country" only a decade ago. San Francisco's famous high-rise Park Merced
development can be seen rearing from an area occupied with the raising of
truck-garden produce and commercial flowers not many years ago.   (*Photo
by Advance-Star and Green Sheet, Burlingame, California*)

34   Sunset Boulevard area, 1922. Somewhat built up now, this subdivision is
called Beverly Hills, California — one of the most expensive pieces of real
estate on earth.   (*Photo by Title Insurance and Trust Company, Los
Angeles, Collection of Historical Photographs*)

35 Tucson, Arizona, starts a suburb in 1954. In next photo see how this lonely little service station (lower left) gets "surrounded" by a supermarket! (*Tucson Sunshine Climate Club photo*)

36 Tucson gets a suburb in 1963! (See if you can find the service station.) (*Tucson Sunshine Climate Club photo*)

37 Ski incline, the superior new ski resort opened at Incline Village, Lake Tahoe, during the winter of 1967. In addition to its ultra-modern facilities, Ski Incline offers ideal skiing for the smallest "Snow Bunny" to the most expert "Schuss-boomer." Developer Arthur Wood is justly proud that excellent snow grooming has kept the accident rate the lowest in the country, a huge inducement for family vacation trade.   *(Photo by Luggi Foeger)*

38 Dave McCoy's new million dollar gondola lift at Mammoth Mountain in California's Sierra Nevada. Gone are the old rope tows. Today nine lifts of various sorts take 4000 skiers a day from the village at 8000 feet up to the breath-taking Alpine slopes at 10,000 feet and higher—and those who ride the new gondola make the ascent in Rolls-Royce comfort! We were asked not to say that the skiing at Mammoth is "unparalleled." (Sorry!) But we can safely say it is superb.

39 A line squall obscures a 2000-acre southwest "subdivision" in dust. So far as we could tell (we were there during a nationwide cold spell—temperature was six degrees above zero) not a soul had attempted to live on his 2½-acre "rancheria." At a service station 38 miles down the road we were told the subdivision straddled the bed of an old dry lake.

40 Lou Tedesco, director of the Miss America Pageant TV show, and his wife, Ann, are shown taking a shoebox full of newly acquired "real estate" back to their Riverside Drive apartment in New York City. The Tedescos purchased ten acres of investment land at Willow Springs in Kern County, California. Upon seeing this photograph Lou called his New York-born wife "The Madonna of the Land." This soil is among the most fertile in the West, with ample water available.

41 Author Leland Frederick Cooley stands beside a stake marking location of USGS survey marker at corner of newly acquired acreage in Southern California's Antelope Valley. Shortly after the Cooley's purchased the land the California Water Project announced the construction of a new 600 acre recreation lake and reservoir just seven miles down the road from here! "Lee" Cooley, a retired pioneer television writer-producer whose credits include the Perry Como Show, the Patti Page Show and a score of other hit musicals, has been a full-time novelist since 1960. Doubleday published his first work, *Run for Home* in 1958. Since then he co-authored *The Retirement Trap* with Mrs. Cooley (1965) and authored four other Doubleday novels, *God's High Table* (1962), *The Richest Poor Folks* (1963), *The Trouble with Heaven* (1966), and *Condition Pink* (1967). Three of his novels have been bought for motion pictures.

42 Co-author Lee Morrison Cooley (Mrs. Leland F.) poses with a very small portion of the total research that went into this book. Mrs. Cooley is a former Broadway dancer and television and motion-picture choreographer whose hobby is also land.

43   The famous North Shore Yacht Club, motel, and residential development at Salton Sea, California. This is a principal water sport and hunting-fishing resort for Southern Californians. When we first traveled through here in the 1930s any man who proposed this sort of development would have been called "off his rocker," or "a dangerous visionary!" This is but one of several multimillion-dollar resort developments. Most of them are on the west shore. All of them are beautifully equipped.   (*Russell Lapp, photographer*)

44   Golfers on front nine of magnificent new 18-hole championship course at Lake Arrowhead, mile-high mountain resort less than two freeway hours from Los Angeles. An outstanding undertaking by the Lake Arrowhead Development Company. Lots are on paved streets with full utilities. The beautiful main lake is a few blocks to the right of this scene. Like Nevada's Incline Village on Lake Tahoe, we rate this among the very best recreational investments in the West.   (*Rothschild photo, Los Angeles*)

45 Aerial shot of the new residential-resort community of Incline Village at Crystal Bay, Lake Tahoe, in Nevada's Washoe County. This modern subdivision with all utilities in and ready for use, including miles of paved streets and sewers, actually covers more area than the cities of Reno and Sparks combined. In the foreground is a cooperative-apartment project under construction. It is being jointly financed by the developer and the U.S. Plywood Corporation.

46 Arthur Wood's careful planning and developing attracted U.S. Plywood to Incline Village. Their Crystal Shores condominiums, shown building above, were sold out faster than they could be completed. Other major quality projects were attracted, among them Rod Campbell's million dollar, thirty unit, resident-owned town-house community, The Cedars. Designed for luxurious year-around living, they are beautifully built, surprisingly reasonable, and add value to the entire area.   *(Photo by Don E. Wolter)*

47   The bean field that became Beverly Hills. The area in the path of the Beverly Hills freeway looked much like this "billion dollar bean field" only a few decades ago. This photo shows part of the Hammel and Denker ranch south of Beverly Hills in the late 1880s. Open farmland comprised most of the development on both sides of the present Santa Monica Freeway right of way until well into the 1920s . . . a perfect example of the slow, inevitable squeeze of our "megaloctopus."   (*Photo from Title Insurance and Trust Company, Los Angeles, Collection of Historical Photos*)

48   Dramatic example of how *people pressure* forces construction of a new freeway through densely populated areas. Here the new Santa Monica Freeway inches its way from the downtown Los Angeles interchange to the Pacific Ocean, visible in the upper left-hand corner. In upper center of picture Beverly Hills, Brentwood, and Bel-Air may be seen. Hollywood may be seen in the upper right-hand corner. Note excavation heading into private dwellings and small business acquired by the state for right of way.   (*Photo by State of California, Department of Public Works, Division of Highways*)

misleading angles in the advertising and sales techniques often used by promoters. We do not say that these are necessarily crooked; they seem to be classic devices. But we do think that you should know what's happening to you before it happens.

The artificial price increase is one device that makes it appear that if you get in on the ground floor, at say $395 for your parcel, you will have shown a whopping increase in a few months when the promoter arbitrarily increases the price of the same sort of parcel in the subdivision by say $200, bringing it to $595 per parcel. If you can believe the old saying, "Land is worth what you can get for it," then perhaps there's a point to be made.

But can *you* sell *your* parcel for the increased figure any time you want to? If you can, then the land has increased in price and you've made a good deal. But chances are that unless you bought "next door to the clubhouse" the subdivider will have a lot of vacant parcels just like yours not far from you and you might have to wait until the area is sold solid before you can move your land for a profit.

It is hard to say just how often these arbitrary increases in price actually do affect the real value of the land. It does seem reasonable though that a promoter would not hike his prices unless he felt that sales were going well enough, and the demand was steady enough, so that he could get away with the increase. If that situation obtains, the increase in your property might be real enough too.

But there's one more thing to watch: The ads might *say* that the price has gone up . . . but the salesmen might also have been instructed to close any deals they can at the old price too, which could be most of the deals they sign. Even at unreasonably high prices there will always be a certain percentage of "moochers," as land salesmen call pushover customers, who will buy *anything* at *any* price . . . on time. Pray for them; they need your help!

One other classic come-on is the "free" lot or the "free" allotment offer.

In the first instance you receive by mail an official-looking letter advising you that "our advertising department has chosen you as one of the fortunate parties to win a free lot in the beautiful new development of Wherezit Acres . . ."

The letter, usually signed by the president himself, then goes on to tell you that if you come to the development within a certain time period (usually short) and bring with you the modest sum of $167.34 "to cover survey and closing costs" you will be given, absolutely free, a clear title to your parcel.

"How lucky can I get?" asked one friend of ours here in Laguna who had just received his notice of free land. When we told him that at least twenty other persons in Laguna alone had also "been chosen" as one of the "fortunate parties" he began to see just how really lucky he was . . . to have met us first. You see, we had taken the $167.34 in cash and gone to collect our free land . . . just to find out what would happen. (We had a pretty good idea because we've been among the "chosen few" before.)

When we got to the inland water resort which had sent out the "come-on" letter we found everything exactly as advertised. There was a club and a motel and stores and gardens and a yacht basin and good food and congenial people and paved streets with all utilities. In fact, it looked even better than in the brochures because the work had been going right ahead.

But when we asked to see the free lot we had won, the nice young sales director grinned a bit sheepishly and said, "I'll show it to you if you really want to see it, but remember . . . there's work to be done there yet." Then he added reassuringly, "It's yours if you *want* it though . . ."

We drove in *his* car (never drive your own) until we came to the end of the pavement. Then we took off across a jeep trail until we came to the middle of a barranca (dry wash) big enough to hide a freight train.

"This was washed through here when the dam busted a few years ago," he explained as we picked our way through house-size boulders. "But it's all surveyed. There won't be any streets here though . . . just easements . . . because the state would not let us include this land in the subdivision containing residential lots" [*proof of the worth of good state laws*].

We looked him square in the eye and asked, "Why do you men, with everything good in the world to point to here at this development, feel that you have to sucker customers all the way down here with this free-lot gimmick?" We told him then that we were writers.

We rode in silence back to the yacht club. Then, over welcome drinks, which he bought, he explained the facts of life in his business. "Look, we're better than 150 miles from the nearest big city. People don't just hop in the family bus and come down here for the happy hell of it! Sure . . . if they did they'd be glad they did . . . [we agreed] but there are so many promoters trying for their attention that we just have to resort to a tried and true gag to get them down here. They may be a little sore at us in the beginning but after we have shown them around and bought them a lunch, they begin to get infected with the activity here. We sell most of them."

We are certain he told us the truth because we stayed overnight and at dinner that night in the yacht-club dining room we met four couples who had come down because of the free lot "come-on" and stayed to purchase residential lots that were far from free. They averaged $5000 each!

Now for the next dodge: If you haven't already received one, it is quite possible that soon you will receive a letter offering you a "free allotment" in some area being developed.

The pitch here is that you may claim the allotment by

appearing on the site on or before a certain specified day in the immediate future at which time you may arrange to receive "full information on the lot set aside, the consideration required, and the privileges granted."

When the cloud of horse feathers settles, it will turn out that the "free allotment" means simply that the promoter is granting you the *right to buy* one of his lots—without charging you for the privilege! Further, you'll find that "consideration" means the price that you must pay for the lot.

It becomes clear then that the purpose of this little gambit is to lure you to the site in order to sell you some land at the *full retail price*. The only thing you've gotten for "nothing" is a good lesson, providing you had sense enough to walk away from the promoter. So the moral of this chapter should be clear: The only effective "land shark" repellent is a great big question mark. Insist upon *full disclosure* of all the facts surrounding and pertinent to the land you are thinking of purchasing and the area it is located in. Remember (especially if you yourself are engaged in the selling game) that when a salesman or an advertising man gets "enthusiastic" or "sold on the deal" himself, he would be less than human if he didn't bend the truth a little! Insist, if you will, that he bend it *your* way—so that you can see it all in focus.

It must be clear by now that solutions—even partial ones —to complex problems are never easy. In the case of land frauds the "rain" of official reproof is very apt to fall upon both the "just and the unjust" alike as the Almighty's rain does in Matthew 5:45.

Oregon's real estate commissioner, Robert J. Jensen, stated the problem from the official point of view when he said before a meeting of the combined realty boards of a number of counties held in Portland's Multnomah Hotel:

"Within the past four years over the United States and in the past one and a half years in Oregon, a problem has arisen to endanger our real estate industry. This is the unscrupulous land promoters. I do not intend giving the impression that all land promoters should be under suspicion, but at this time the reputable and the disreputable are lumped together in the eyes of the suspicious public. Too, the public cannot distinguish between the unlicensed land promoter and the competent real estate licensee."

It might be well to repeat once again that the purpose of this book is to help the average small land investor make that distinction in the hope that one day real estate laws will be beefed up to provide the average buyer with maximum practical protection.

In talking with real estate commissioners, assistant commissioners, realty boards, district attorneys, and attorney generals in various states, it seems clear that one of the most difficult things facing the state legislatures who must enact new laws to meet the new land-promoter threat is to make those laws as "fair, just, and equitable" as they insist the land promoter's deals be.

In all fairness, nobody can say that any given piece of land will not increase in value. But, as we've said, there is always an element of gamble in a land purchase . . . whether it be called an investment or a speculation. The only way to minimize that element is to inform yourself fully with every available fact. It is our hope that this book will make it easier for you to do that by showing you *where* to look and *with whom* to talk.

The spirit of the law and the letter of the law may at times seem to be at odds. No law in its literal application is ever completely just. That is why a set of laws stringent enough to be positive controls on the man whose ethics in land dealings are questionable may, at times, work an unintended hardship on the landman whose ethics are actually above reproach. Law is a living entity, not a static thing. One look at our Constitution will tell you that. With amendments always possible to make that remarkable document meet the growing needs of our society, it is one of the most vital documents ever devised by man. And still, in its attempt to be always just, its Fifth Amendment has made it possible for unethical men to take advantage of its intent and gain protection under the same provision intended by our founding fathers to shield ethical men who may have been unjustly set upon.

In Arizona we spent almost a day searching for a subdivision we'll call, "Blank Springs," that advertised itself as being only minutes from the railroad and industrial center of Kingman. Once located, it proved remote and, to us, worthless. However, another subdivision, literally only minutes from Kingman (five to twenty at the most) would seem to be a promising long-range investment.

We refer to Chrystal Collins' Sun-West Acres and Paradise Acres. Sun-West is divided into twenty acre parcels of unimproved (except for access roads) land. Paradise Acres is subdivided into unimproved one quarter and two-and-one-half acre homesites.

Not only are they easy to locate, they are virtually unavoidable if one enters Kingman from the west or south on the main roads. Says blonde Miss Collins who wears her bikini or her Phi Beta Kappa key with equal grace, *"We are not building a city because we already have one!"*

Indeed, the industrial-rail center of Kingman seems likely to overrun the 14,000 Collins acres. Recently there has been a boom in copper mining in the area. The Duval Corporation's facilities are reportedly valued at $28 million. El Paso Natural Gas is developing a multimillion-dollar mining operation. General Cable plans a $10 million plant and Mid-West Wax Paper has a plant nearby. But for those who invest *without* investigating, "Blank Springs" may sound as attractive as Sun-West or Paradise Acres—*in the ads, that is!*

Most of the government people seemed pessimistic about the land promoters' chances of cleaning up their own profession. The consensus seemed to be that it is well-nigh impossible to change a man's ways once he has found a formula for getting large amounts of money easily from the public.

Oregon's Commissioner Jensen, in a letter to us, says:

"It is my firm belief that each state should have a strong subdivision law to prevent the unscrupulous from selling marginal or worthless land to the unsuspecting. With few exceptions these offerings are made to induce the elderly on pension, the working man on a small salary, or the overseas veteran looking toward retirement. In each instance these classes of people are looking for some means of implementing their incomes and the dangling by the developer of possible wealth through investment is more than these unsuspecting people can resist. . . ."

It is only fair to point out the vast difference between a highly developed community such as Havasu City, remote though it may be, and crude "unanchored subdivisions" that have plagued real estate commissioners in most of the western states. At Havasu City the vital industrial nucleus is built-in. In few other areas is it even nearby.

In all of the states in which raw desert land is being subdivided and offered for sale, there are fine new communities which give promise of healthy growth and increase in value within reasonable periods of time. Also, unfortunately, in some states there are "bare minimum" or substandard promotions that should never be dignified by the name "development." Most of these cannot possibly increase in real value to anywhere near their actual sales prices for perhaps a generation or more, population explosion notwithstanding. They are too far off the beaten track to take immediate advantage of the well-established growth pattern of the strip city. It may be that a few of them will, in time, see a presently unpredictable growth because they will have been fortunate enough to have been located near some newly discovered mining area or some newly established government installation which will create an "island" of development. But in gambler's parlance, "That's really bucking the odds!"

So, it must be clear that the problem is a difficult one for both the lawmakers who want to protect the gullible and still be fair with the ethical developers, and for the developers themselves who must risk millions on their judgment and who cannot, in all honesty, say that despite a remarkable collective record of successes their judgment is always infallible.

Much as a tightrope walker must teeter precariously until he gets his balance and can negotiate his thin line, it seems to us that the law will have to lean mightily toward total protection while the land developers will have to struggle to counterbalance with equal vigor by policing their recalcitrant members who make stringent laws necessary. Perhaps by compromises—*practical ones on both sides*—the practices of the unethical few can be effectively stopped without seriously restricting the land-developing industry as a whole. The best of these developers represent the best of private enterprise. They have the machinery and the know-how to provide for the orderly expansion of our urban, suburban, and recreational needs. If the malpractices of the few make it impossible for the many to operate, free enterprise will have sustained another serious blow.

Just as the real estate brokers got together to form the National Board of Realtors and set ethical standards for their member realtors, so perhaps must the land developers now expand the pioneer move being made by a few groups. If the great majority of western land developers can band together into a national group and subscribe to a code of ethics and adhere to it or be discredited, then a great part of the reason for supertough all embracing laws will have been removed. Perhaps then a few very specific and essentially just laws can be enacted that will impose deserved penalties on the dedicated crooks and borderline operators in the business.

Being realistic about the limitations of homo sapiens we are moved to opine that it may take men with the tenacity and courage of Lassie and Rin-Tin-Tin and the judgment of Solomon to bring this about. But it's all to the good that a start has been made.

10

HOW LAND IS MEASURED, DIVIDED, AND LOCATED

The orderly location, division, and subdivision of land as we know it today did not always exist. In fact, accurate maps upon which men could locate their land to within inches of its exact boundaries sort of grew, like Topsy. And very often in the growing process, Topsy was plenty turvy.

As America's increasing population began flowing outward in small trickles from harbors along its eastern coastline, and these trickles became swelling streams of migration that eventually would overflow our country, the pioneers began to "take up" land in places that appealed to them.

In the beginning, except for the Crown Colonies of England, France, and Spain, which had been roughly bounded and parceled in the original charter surveys, the process of "taking up" land meant simply that a man cleared as much of it as he could work. By right of occupancy it became his. If and when others settled near him or next to him, boundaries were established by mutual agreement, monuments, natural or man-made, were designated at corners, and crude maps were drawn.

When enough people settled to form a community, those crude maps were often recorded or placed on record with the early town authorities so that a man's right and title to his particular parcel of land could be confirmed in the event of dispute, in the event of sale or transfer of title to all or part of it, or in the event of the need to accurately identify the land as part of an estate after the death of the title holder of record.

There are some fascinating books available if one wishes to explore the history of land allotment and homesteading.[1] And there are some classic brannigans over boundaries and some attempted land swindles which, for sheer brutality or ingenuity, probably have not been surpassed anywhere in the world.

We can think of one, for instance, in which a resident of Mexico City, one Don Jose Limantour, appeared before the California Land Commission in 1853 with papers purporting to prove that over a half a million acres south of San Francisco, including a big slice of the city itself, were really his by right of a grant from the Spanish Crown. Limantour produced old papers, complete with impressive seals and signatures. He also produced the necessary witnesses. After a thorough hearing the Land Commission decided his claim was valid. Immediately crowds of people, who up until then thought they had clear title to their land, began clamoring to give Limantour and his agents varying sums of money in return for the quitclaim deeds needed to quiet title, as it is called.

The records show that Limantour thus collected better than a quarter of a million dollars—some say a half a million

[1] *Dreamers of the American Dream* by Stuart Holbrook for one.

—before new evidence came to light which tended to indicate that a lot of key testimony and exhibits might not have
been on the level.

A group of landholders who had paid Limantour for
quitclaim deeds hired investigators who discovered that the
whole thing was a beautifully engineered swindle. Witnesses had been paid to bend the truth, and papers and seals
had been forged. But Don Jose Limantour, equipped with a
burgeoning bag of gold, had left on an extended tour south
of the border, down Mexico way. He seems to have lived
happily ever after!

The so-called Limantour grant was not the only such
misadventure in clouded California land titles back in the
1850s when the Land Commission was busy processing something in excess of 500 such sticky title claims. A little later
in this chapter when we talk about title companies and their
functions in more detail you'll see why, with our western
land especially, it is an absolute necessity to have a clear
title established and insured. Though it may seem a bit like
fiction today—160 years or so later—there are still areas in the
West where these old land grants are a potential source of
confusion and trouble.

Back in the 1850s a great many disputes centered around
the fixing of valid boundaries on ranchos that were subsequently sold in whole or in part. The surveys were very informal in those days. Great distances were measured in
leagues, which were approximately three miles in length.
Often their length varied with the country that used them.

A fine example of the informal practices of the times may
be read in the informative little booklet, *Pinning Down Your
Property* published by the California Land Title Association
and distributed by the Title Insurance and Trust Company
in Los Angeles among others. Under the heading, "Oldtime
Measuring Practices," it says in part:

Back in the days when California was principally vast open land—and the land was of little value—it mattered little that boundaries of areas generally were vaguely determined. If a portion of someone's holdings were to be specified in granting grazing rights, or when an area was to be sold or given to some ranchero, the methods were, by today's standards, crude and curious.

Old records refer to such landmarks as "the dead oak tree with the skull of a steer set in its fork," "the clump of sycamores springing from one root"—boundary line markers which, with passing years disappeared forever. Stones, houses, adobe walls, streams—reference points of many kinds—were used, often with little apparent regard for the fact that time might erase them as markers, or that their location might be changed.

To measure distances from such then-recognizable points, the surveyors' methods varied. Two men on horseback might drag a cord, or rawhide thong line, of say, 100 varas length (a vara being approximately 33 inches), one standing while the other rode ahead, and then riding on past his helper, turn by turn and counting their line lengths. Or, the circumference of the wheel of a cart would be measured; with that as a unit, and a thong tied to a spoke so that the wheel's revolutions might be tallied, a rider would drive over the hill and valley and report the "exact" dimensions of the land.

It is easy to see now, however, in this day of strip cities and densely populated megalopolises that no such informal methods would do. With some land worth as much as $20,000 a *square foot* the error of half an inch along one side of such a parcel would be a $792 mistake. In the days of our great-grandmothers, $792 would have bought a square mile (one section) of good bottom land. Times *have* changed!

The problem of these casually established boundaries was not California's alone. It was general over most of the West; most particularly where the generous, open-handed Spaniards and Mexicans had taken up the land by exploration and by conquest from the primitive natives.

The law of supply and demand has forced us, step by step, to place greater and greater value on our dwindling supply of developable land. As the price has gone up so has the interest of the purchaser who wants to make sure nobody's shaving a half inch off his side line. A woman who buys an ounce of perfume for $30 is a lot more concerned with whether the bottle is full to the top than the woman who buys a pint of cheap toilet water for $3.00. So who cares if *that* bottle is a teaspoonful light? But precious land—and that's *all* land today—must be meticulously measured, described, and recorded. If you think that it is an exaggeration to say that "all land is precious today" just stop a moment and ponder these figures: Every minute 100 more persons are being added to the earth's population according to Vogt in his book, *The People.* That means 6000 new persons every hour—144,000 persons every 24 hours—4,320,000 persons every month—51,840,000 persons every 12 months.

In the western states alone it has been estimated that three quarters of a million new people come searching for new homes each year—and that doesn't count the constant stream of new "native sons and daughters" that come squalling onto the scene each day.

We have purposely tried to keep too many figures—too many "nuts and bolts"—out of this book, preferring to illustrate our points by using true stories. But we have come to that part of the book now where we must indulge in a little elementary "technical talk" so that you will be acquainted with the basic terms you'll hear when you go to talk to your real estate man.

It is likely that you'll know most of the words. After all,

you have probably bought your home, which is located on a lot, which in turned is located in a city block, which in turn is located in a tract of your city.

If you hold a trust deed or a grant deed, your property is probably described as being, say, Lot 11, Block 4, Tract 7117 in the Township of "Somethingorother."

But, if you already own raw acreage that has not been subdivided into residential plots or parcels, then you know that the description must be a little more basic or elementary because you are trying to pin down your particular piece of some larger portion of our rapidly vanishing wide-open spaces. Let's get acquainted with how this pinning down process works. Once you know that, by the way, it will make your own picnics, your own hikes, your own rockhound trips, or whatever, much more fascinating because you'll be expecting and probably finding some of the United States Coast and Geodetic Survey markers or "monuments" from which all of our land is measured.

Roughly speaking, land areas in the United States are divided into TOWNSHIPS, SECTIONS, FRACTIONS OF SECTIONS, AND PARCELS OF SMALLER ACREAGE.

For the sake of simplicity look at the drawings that accompany this text. They will help you visualize the divisions of land. It's really very easy and logical and needn't confuse you at all. It is a matter of dividing up some basic squares.

To keep it absolutely simple, let's invent a *square state* called "West Utopia." Let's make it 60 miles square, which means it will contain 3600 square miles (60 × 60).

Obviously one could eventually locate a parcel of land in this relatively small area by counting east or west or north or south from these ideal borders.

Each of the squares indicated in the sketch (we have arbitrarily said there are 100 of them in West Utopia) represents a *township* . . . a major division of land.

Each of these square townships is *6 miles square* and con-

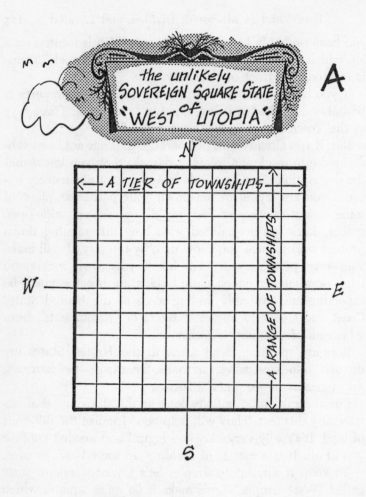

the unlikely
SOVEREIGN SQUARE STATE
"WEST of UTOPIA"

A

N

← A TIER OF TOWNSHIPS →

A RANGE OF TOWNSHIPS

W —————————————— E

S

N

A TOWNSHIP =
36 SECTIONS

1 mile

1 mile

ONE SECTION 6	5	4	3	2	1
7	8	9	10	11	12
18	17	16	15	14	13
19	20	21	22	23	24
30	29	28	27	26	25
31	32	33	34	35	36

W

E

6 miles

6 miles

S

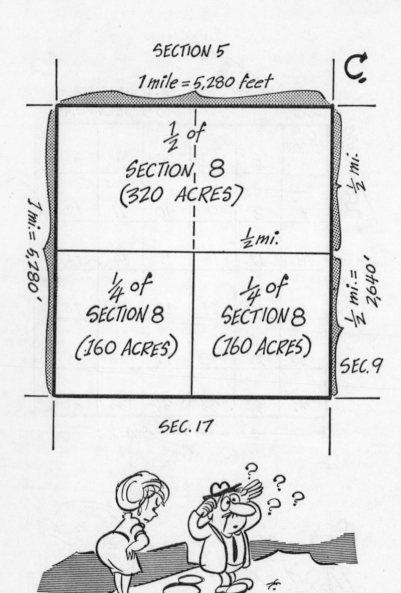

tains 36 square miles of land (6 × 6). You use the same arithmetic employed to figure the number of square feet in your living room.

Each of the 36 square-mile units of land in a township is called a *section. A section is one square mile.* It is also *one mile square.* In other words, a section measures one mile along each of its four sides. It is usually considered to be an absolute square.

So, in each township, there are 36 sections, each measuring one square mile.

Each of these sections is given a number, beginning with 1 in the upper right hand corner of the township and continuing westward to section number 6, then dropping down south and picking up with section 7, then proceeding eastward again to section 12 and so on, back and forth, until all 36 sections have been numbered in the individual township.

This section, which is one mile square, is broken up into smaller subdivisions known as *half sections* and *quarter sections.*

A *section* contains 640 acres of land

A *half-section* contains 320 acres of land

A *quarter-section* contains 160 acres of land

Smaller pieces of land within a section, that is parcels of less than *one-quarter section,* or 160 acres, are usually referred to by the numbers of acres they contain. For example, an 80-acre *parcel,* a 40-acre *parcel,* a 20-acre *parcel,* a 10-acre *parcel,* a 5-acre *parcel,* a 2½-acre *parcel* . . . or any fractional divisions of any of those.

If you'll look carefully at the next drawing you'll see the way a section of land, 640 acres, may be broken down.

Now then, knowing some of the names and identities of the pieces or parcels of land we may be looking for, let's find out how to locate them. To do this, we'll return for a mo-

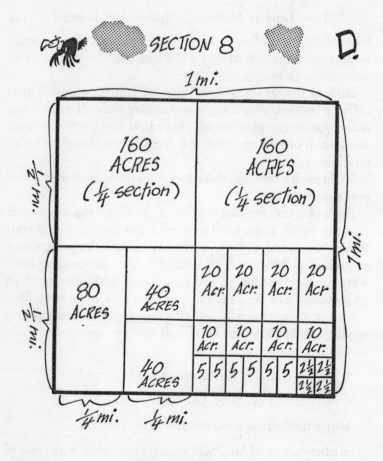

SECTION 8   D.

1 mi.

160 ACRES (¼ section)	160 ACRES (¼ section)

½ mi.   1 mi.

80 ACRES | 40 ACRES | 20 Acr. | 20 Acr. | 20 Acr. | 20 Acr

½ mi.

| | | 10 Acr. | 10 Acr. | 10 Acr. | 10 Acr. |

40 ACRES | 5 | 5 | 5 | 5 | 5 | 5 | 2½ | 2½ |
          | | | | | | | 2½ | 2½ |

¼ mi.   ¼ mi.

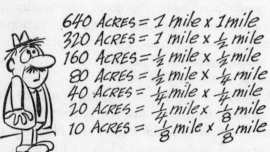

640 ACRES = 1 mile x 1 mile
320 ACRES = 1 mile x ½ mile
160 ACRES = ½ mile x ½ mile
80 ACRES = ½ mile x ¼ mile
40 ACRES = ¼ mile x ¼ mile
20 ACRES = ¼ mile x ⅛ mile
10 ACRES = ⅛ mile x ⅛ mile

ment to our basic division of land, the *township*, which contains 36 sections of one square mile each.

Obviously the first thing to do in searching for a bit of land is to locate the township it is in.

The U.S. Coast and Geodetic Survey has made that fairly easy by dividing up our mythical state of West Utopia into a whole mess of townships, all of them identified as being north or south or east or west of certain arbitrary lines which for practical purposes parallel the earth's own lines of latitude and which, in the United States at least, may be said also for practical purposes, to be parallel north and south too. However, any school boy or girl knows that the meridians of longitude are not actually parallel because they are inscribed on a globe and must converge at the North and South poles. If the engineers didn't make allowances and corrections to work within practical limits, a section of land touching the North or South poles would wind up being a triangle— a king-size slice of frozen custard pie. But don't get cagey now and start looking for *your* section of land on the equator, feeling you'll get a better bargain. You won't. A section of land, where we North Americans will likely be buying it, will be one mile square no matter where it is!

If you will look at our drawing of West Utopia for a moment now, the following explanation will become very simple.

The two arbitrary lines of location are the *meridian line* that bisects our state north and south . . . and the *base line* which bisects it east and west.

Each of the squares (townships) is located by saying it lies north or south or east or west of one of these two arbitrary location lines.

Now look at the drawing again and you'll notice that the north-south columns of townships are called *ranges* and the east-west rows of townships are called *tiers*.

Knowing this and knowing the system of numbering them,

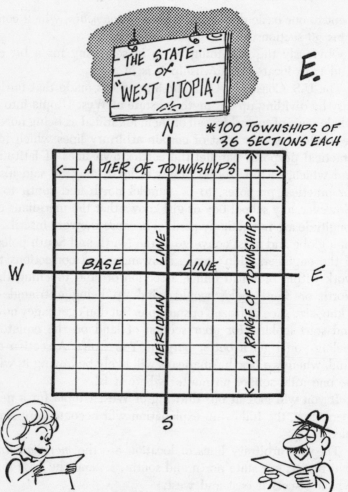

THE STATE OF "WEST UTOPIA"

E.

N

* 100 TOWNSHIPS OF 36 SECTIONS EACH

← A TIER OF TOWNSHIPS →

BASE LINE LINE

MERIDIAN LINE

A RANGE OF TOWNSHIPS

W   E

S

* "WEST UTOPIA" HAS 100 TOWNSHIPS FOR OUR CON- VENIENCE ONLY. ACTUALLY A STATE HAS AS MANY TOWNSHIPS AS IT HAS ROOM FOR 36 MILE SQUARE DIVISIONS OF ITS LAND. NATURALLY, BECAUSE OF IRREGULAR BORDER LINES, THE PERIPHERAL TOWN- SHIPS MAY NOT BE COMPLETE ONES.

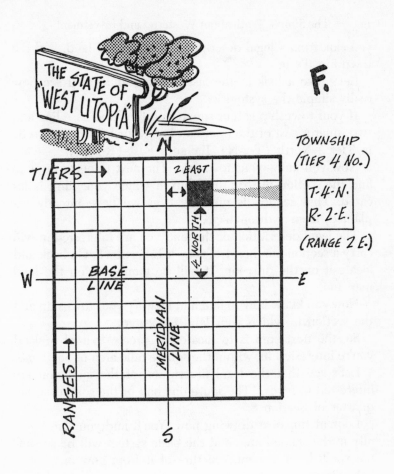

F.

TOWNSHIP
(TIER 4 No.)

T-4-N.
R-2-E.

(RANGE 2 E.)

you can, from a legal description of a piece of land, find the township it's in.

Let's take a look at the last drawing and you'll see how really simple the system is:

If your township is four squares north of the base line and two squares east of the meridian line, your land is said to be in Tier 4 North (T-4-N), Range 2 East (R-2-E).

Now you know your township. The next thing to do is to find the section in that township in which your land is located. That section is numbered, as we have already explained, from 1 through 36.

The legal description of the land you are interested in will carry a section number. Let's say it is Section 8. Go back and locate it on the drawing. It will be numbered on the land map too.

Now you know how to find and identify your township and the section in which your land is located.

So, the next step is to locate the precise parcel of land you're interested in, within the square mile area of Section 8.

Let's say that the legal description of the land you are interested in reads, "The south one half of the southeast one quarter of Section 8."

Look at this next drawing now. You'll find your land in a jiffy in the shaded area and the basic system will be so simple you'll keep a mental picture of it from now on.

You'll see that the piece of land you are interested in is actually a half of a quarter section, or 80 acres, and that may be more than you can afford, even in good raw land.

Let's say you can only manage 10 acres now. Alright, we'll show you how to find that 10 acres. Let's make up a typical legal description of it so you can trace it and "pin it down" exactly in "Township Four north-Two east."

Your 10 acres is described legally as being (don't get worried now!), "The southeast one quarter of the southeast one quarter of the southeast one quarter of Section 8." Believe it

49   The Goldwyn Studios in Culver City, California, in the early 1920s. Note old movie sets standing along unpaved "street" at right. This studio, now M.G.M., invaded the bean fields. The "megaloctopus" has engulfed it. The land may now be too valuable for movie-making. Consequently M.G.M. and other major studios are exploring the possibility of constructing a consolidated *cinema city* in the Malibu Mountains north of Beverly Hills, where land may still be bought for four figures by the acre, not by the front foot!

50   "Mayor" Will Rogers returns from New York theatrical appearances to be welcomed as chief official of Beverly Hills, California, in the early 1920s. Mrs. Rogers may be seen holding bouquet beneath "Home to thaw out" sign. Film star Conrad Nagel and Mrs. Nagel may be seen directly in back of Will Rogers. These were the halcyon days of silent films and noisy Southern California civic promotions. Many a crowded old-timer mourns their passing!   (*Photo from Title Insurance and Trust Company, Los Angeles, Collection of Historical Photographs*)

51   Washington State's dramatic new North Cross-state Highway pushes westward up Early Winters Canyon toward the Pacific Slope ports of Anacortes and Seattle on the far side of the Cascades. When completed around 1968 this new highway will end a period of comparative isolation for the immensely rich Methow and upper Okanogan valleys in north-central Washington. Here is a classic long-range land-investment situation in the making. In the novel, *God's High Table*, the Jakobites, who opposed this highway, packed down this canyon's rugged trail to trade with the despised sinners in "Mill City" (Twisp). (*Photo by Dick Webb*)

52   The town of Twisp (Indian for "yellow jacket") is the commercial heart of the vast Washington lumbering, mining, agricultural, and cattle-ranching complex of the Methow Valley. It is also one of the world's finest hunting and fishing areas. Washington's breath-taking Lake Chelan resort area lies just below the southern end of Methow, pronounced "*met*-how."   (*Photo by Dick Webb*)

53 A small portion of Lake Havasu City as seen from the new Nautical Inn. This 16,520 acre master-planned community is one of the largest in the country. A gentle sloping rise of three degrees eastward from Lake Havasu shoreline offers a lake view from virtually every area of the city. By the time this McCulloch Corporation development was 40 months old, over $31 million had been invested in homes, apartments, businesses, construction, engineering, recreational facilities and other improvements. Over 2000 residents have settled here. Scores of others fly in from all over the United States on Lake Havasu's private fleet of Lockheed Constellations, operating six to eight scheduled flights each week.

54 Eighteenth hole of Hesperia (California) Golf Course showing the finish
of a P.G.A. tournament. On these high-desert western courses golfers and
"hackers" may pray and cuss 365 days a year.

55 Fairways and spring-fed ponds at Alta Sierra, Wolf Creek, California, a new residential and vacation development in the heart of the famed '49 country. Midway between Sacramento and Lake Tahoe, and adjacent to new super-freeways, Alta Sierra is a classic example of "people pressure" forcing development out along the tentacles of a growing megaloctopus. A decade ago land such as this was less than $200 an acre. Today it runs as high as $200 a front foot!

56 Well Number Four at Christmas Valley development in central Oregon pumps 2300 gallons per minute. Oldtimers and some authorities contend that the annual rainfall in this arid central region is insufficient to replenish the underground reservoirs being tapped by these new developments if all the people who have purchased come to live on their land. History has shown, however, that when an area outgrows its indigenous water supply ways are usually found to bring in water from nearby areas with an oversupply. Like all of our western states, Oregon's water problem is not one of supply but of distribution.

57 First Southern Pacific train breaks "Barrier" as new 78 mile Palmdale-Colton (California) cut-off is dedicated, July 11, 1967. *(See map below)*

58 S.P.'s new Palmdale-Colton line opens attractive new industrial sites in two fast growing areas in Southern California. The Colton-San Bernardino area, already well developed, is destined for still more growth because of increased distribution flexibility. The Palmdale-Lancaster area, located at the Los Angeles gateway to the Antelope Valley is on the threshold of a tremendous expansion. This first new American rail line in twenty-five years will provide dynamic impetus to growth already stimulated by the new Antelope Valley Freeway and by the imminent arrival of the $2 billion California Water Project. By constructing this new line the Southern Pacific has completed a classic new design for progress! *(Map courtesy S.P.R.R.)*

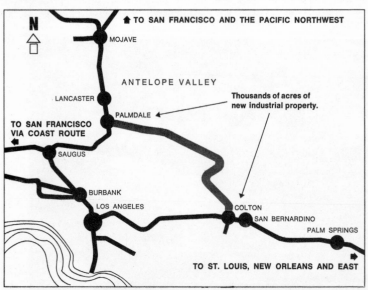

59 Riverside, California, from Mount Rubidoux shortly after 1900. Note profusion of trees as described in 1880s by Grandfather Stephens. New neo-classic City Hall can be seen in left center of picture.

60 Riverside, California, in 1963. Its population went from 46,764 in 1950 to 84,332 in 1960. The freeway linking Long Beach, Los Angeles, San Diego, and way points to Riverside, Redlands, and San Bernardino is seen snaking through the photo. In the distance are the remains of the great sea of orange groves which covered the metropolitan area when Grandfather Stephens bought here in 1883. Arrow shows same city hall today.   *(Photo by Fred Bauman, Riverside Press Enterprise & Riverside Chamber of Commerce)*

California City, May, 1959
with first recreation unit
and start of business and
residential construction.

61   California City, May 1959, with first recreation unit and start of business
and residential construction. This engineering is a far cry from the rough
"ranch roads" shown in some of the previous photos in this book.

62   Colorado City, sister community to California City. Here, a scant three
years after ground was broken, a beautiful golf course challenges the scores
of new residents, a portion of whose homes may be seen bordering the fairway.
Out of the picture to the left lies Lake Beckwith which boasts a new pavilion
and small boat marina . . . and quite probably some of the best fishing in the
state.

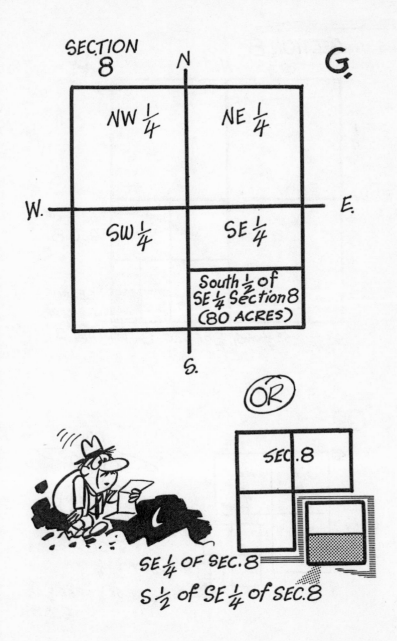

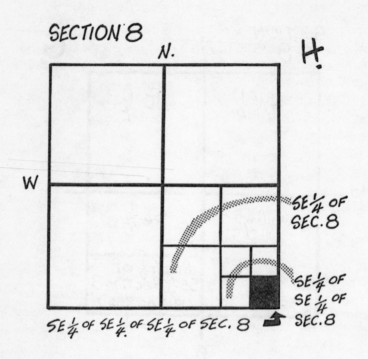

SECTION 8

N.

H.

W

SE ¼ OF SEC.8

SE ¼ OF SE ¼ OF SEC.8

SE ¼ OF SE ¼ OF SE ¼ OF SEC. 8

OR

| NW ¼ | NE ¼ |
| SW ¼ | |

SE ¼

SE ¼ OF SE ¼

SE ¼ OF SE ¼ OF SE ¼ OF SEC.8

or not, that is your 10 acres! It's the corner 10 acres, shown in the shaded area. The trick is to keep on dividing squares into squares or tandem squares (rectangles) until you've got your land fenced in.

Let's do another practice problem and locate the 10 acres that touch *your northwest corner*. You don't know the legal description on it so you are going to reason it out by looking at the plat (the map of the section or half section). Draw it up yourself. You don't need a printed map to do this.

Obviously that other 10-acre parcel is still in the southeast quarter of the southeast quarter of Section 8. But what part of the southeast quarter of the southeast quarter is it? Well, if you don't lose your direction, it's the *northwest* quarter of the southeast quarter of the southeast quarter of Section 8. And that's all there is to it.

Now of course if you were trying to pin down an *irregular* piece of land of fractional acreage you'd use a slightly more complicated drawing but the same simple principle applies.

Let's do one just for fun. We say "just for fun" because we find this game of locating land a lot easier than a cross-word puzzle—and a lot more profitable!

Look at this next drawing now. Quite probably you have figured out how to keep dividing up squares until you've got it pinned down. But let's do it anyway. The piece we want to identify by its correct legal description is an L-shaped 30-acre parcel in the southeast one quarter of Section 8.

Don't look at the land as one 30-acre parcel. Look at it as *three* contiguous 10-acre parcels, each located in a different quarter of the southeast quarter of the section. That will make you see the sub-squares more readily.

So, we could start with the parcel marked #1. It is the southwest one quarter of the northeast one quarter of the southeast one quarter of Section 8.

The parcel marked #2 is the northeast one quarter of

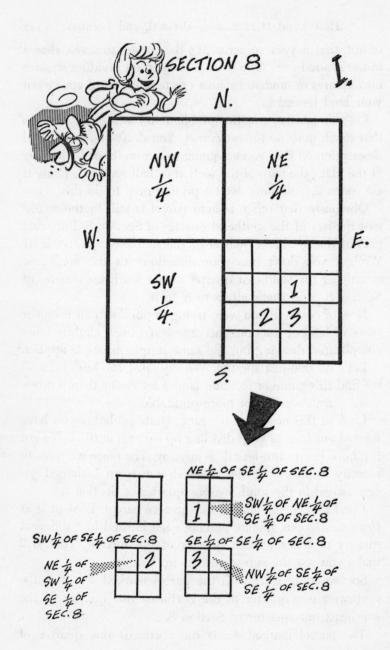

the southwest one quarter of the southeast one quarter of Section 8.

The parcel marked #3 is the northwest one quarter of the southeast one quarter of the southeast one quarter of Section 8.

It's a tough one if you have to type it ten times on copies of deeds or title reports, but otherwise it's really not difficult.

Theoretically you can keep squaring land down to 1 acre or 1/640 of a section.

Certainly there are still tougher applications of the location principle and there are some situations where the simple squaring method won't work. If, for instance, you need to isolate a piece of land that is 3.7 acres in area, a far more complicated set of legal descriptions is necessary and a very precise survey. But a good land surveyor, starting with the township monuments and the section monuments, can pinpoint the smallest piece of land exactly. These men work miracles with their rods, chains, and transits. If it weren't for them there'd be no such thing as friendly neighbors—only angry enemies. (Remember the cave man who staked out his real estate holdings with a club? Obviously the man with the biggest club held the most land. Sometimes in this world it seems that the system hasn't really changed too much, doesn't it?)

Well—we've come down from a mythical state, through its townships and its sections to its parcels of acres.

The next question is: How large is an acre?

Acres can be of various shapes but not of various sizes; they always remain 1/640 of a section (1/640 of 1 square mile). An acre always contains 43,560 square feet. If it is in a square it will measure 208.71 feet (208 feet 8½ inches) along each side.

If you wanted to step off an approximate acre on a parcel of raw land, you could take 69½ 3-foot steps straight ahead, then take a like number at a right angle to the left or right,

SOME BASIC LAND DIVISIONS

J.

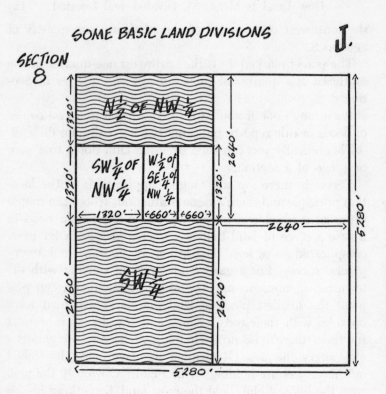

SECTION 8

N ½ OF NW ¼

SW ¼ OF NW ¼

W ½ of SE ¼ of NW ¼

SW ¼

1320'
1320'
2460'
5280'
1320'
2640'
1320'
2640'
2640'
1320'
660'
660'
2640'
5280'

SURVEYORS' LINGO
80 CHAINS TO A MILE
(66' = 1 CHAIN)

40 CHAINS
20 CH.
10 C.
5 C.
5 C.
80 CHAINS

and keep on doing that until you returned to your starting point. You would have stepped off an approximate square acre. It's a fair-sized piece of real estate. If you own it free and clear in the right place, you and your family won't have to worry much about that Hawaiian vacation or the new car or new mink stole.

There are acres of other shapes, too, but they all contain the same 43,560 square feet.

If you have 50-foot frontage an acre will run back 871.2 feet.

If you have 75-foot frontage an acre will run back 580.8 feet.

If you have 100-front feet your acre will run back 435.6 feet.

If you have 150-front feet your acre will run back 290.4 feet.

And there are still more variations, of course.

Let's put in one more land diagram, using the section as the basic unit. We don't have to answer any questions about how long a basic piece of land is; it's all right in the drawing. You'll find it useful too.

11

"THE LAY OF THE LAND"

We were very careful to include the word "simple" in the title of this book because it is intended as a primer or "first reader" for the average person who has had little or no experience in the location and purchase of land for investment or speculation.

We know of no investment or speculation that offers more rewarding fun and excitement in the seeking of it—or more potential profit—than the finding and buying of a good parcel of raw land. But—as we've said earlier—today land is not an investment that the amateur should attempt to make all by himself.

The list of thirteen questions which the National Better Business Bureau suggests you ask before purchasing must have given you some idea of the traps that you can get into unless you employ the services of a licensed broker or realtor and also, in states where it is possible, *take the precaution of using the services of a good title insurance firm.*

In short, the first mark to put on any land contract or other land-purchase agreement offered you is a *question mark.*

Since we are primarily concerned with larger pieces of undeveloped or semideveloped investment land, it's not necessary to go into the tract, block, and lot subdivisions . . . unless you happen to be considering acreage in an old subdivision. As we've said before, your home probably occupies a portion of one such if you live in an incorporated town, in a city, or in a suburb.

Even if you live on a parcel of land considerably larger than the usual city lot, you may find that the county surveyor's map will show your property to be in a tract. That may have happened many years ago when land was far more plentiful and some promoter whacked up a few sections of land into rather large pieces which were recorded as tracts. Usually such a tract will bear the original subdivider's name. Quite often, too, a fairly large parcel of land will be found to have once been a part of a much larger subdivision of land.

In looking at county surveyors' maps in several western states, we have found literally dozens of variations of the tract and subdivision designations. Many "lots" were as large as 20 acres in the days of plentiful land. The responsibility of dividing the land was left to the discretion of the local or county authorities. In many cases these good men could not possibly have foreseen the day when "all that worthless land" would suddenly be the most valuable investment a buyer could have made.

In most states now, certain minimum requirements have to be met before land is subdivided for sale. The requirements vary greatly.

But you may be looking at land which was whacked up into small pieces before the new laws went into effect. Since the laws may not be retroactive, your particular parcel may not be subject to their protection. A good example of what we mean is the current rash of indictments against allegedly unethical subdividers who are said to have misrepresented such basic things as their legal right to sell you the land in the first place! Protection against that? *Those questions again!*

Now then, let's take some random examples of how land is packaged for sale.

You know about city lots. You know something about 2½-acre parcels which are often advertised as being "equal to ten city lots."

One and a quarter and 2½-acre subdivisions are among the most popular in the West today. They are among the most dangerous, too, because of the laxity of some state laws authorizing them. But, it must be said in all fairness that they can be potentially good investments if purchased properly— and in the proper place.

Many of the subdividers who create 2½-acre "Record of Survey" subdivisions (rough-graded roads, minimum drainage, and seldom any utilities) use the "ten city lots" pitch in their advertising.

We have asked many of them why they do this when they know that before a 2½-acre parcel may be broken up into ten city lots, "one hell of a lot of things have to happen!" as one state official put it. "It helps the folks visualize the size of their property," is nearly always the answer of the subdividers.

Actually, it may—if you know the size of "an average city lot." But it seems more likely to us that the line is used to induce in the buyer a mental picture of the fantastic profits he might make from subdividing his 2½ acres into ¼-acre lots.

Believe us, even if it made sense it isn't as easy as all that today! First, under new laws you'd have to go through a long, complicated, and expensive process of filing an intention to subdivide, then you'd have to employ engineers to go over the land to make a feasibility study and give you cost estimates; you'd have to comply with all of the zoning in effect for your type of subdivision, which could mean the construction of streets, sewers, storm drains and the bringing in of all utilities to your lots. Before you got into the first day of preparations, unless you're an exceptional person indeed, you'd throw up your hands in holy horror and wait until a professional subdivider came along buying up land all around you. *Then* is when you'd make a fine profit on your $2\frac{1}{2}$-acre parcel . . . if you paid a fair price for it in the first place. But the "big money" is usually made by the professional men who subdivide large tracts of land. They can take advantage of the "quantity discount" and the standardization of procedures and materials, something the "little guy" cannot do.

Of course if you hang on with grim determination until you are surrounded by shopping centers and high-rise office buildings like folks in Las Vegas, Phoenix, Tucson, and Albuquerque did . . . and especially folks in California's San Fernando and Antelope valleys . . . then you will almost certainly make a "killing." One farmer-turned-realtor in Lancaster, California, is a wealthy man today because he did just that. His name is Alvin Hartwig. As this is being revised he has sold out and retired. He's been president of just about every civic organization in the Emerald Triangle of the Antelope Valley.

When we interviewed him recently he told us an amusing story. Because its moral is obvious, we want to tell it to you.

"When I came here to the Antelope Valley in 1945," Al said, "I was determined to settle on some of its land. Well, it took a little while to find a piece I could afford but I finally found a 40-acre piece with a house and some barns and things on it, so I bought it. It was just west of town."

Hartwig grinned at a private recollection, then went on in

his engaging Alabama drawl. "Anyway, I went to a stock auction one day to get me a herd bull. 'Course I was a stranger and folks didn't know me. Well, I was leaning up against the corral fence waiting for the auction to start when I overheard two fellas talking. One of them said, 'I hear somebody just bought that rundown old 40-acre place west of town.' The second fella said, 'Oh? 'Zat so . . . ? Who'd ever waste money on that place?' The first man replied, 'Oh, I dunno . . . some out-of-state sucker, I s'pose!' "

Al Hartwig leaned back against the fender of his new Rolls-Royce and chuckled amiably.

"That old run-down place made a living for me and my family. It was west of town when I bought it . . . but you might say it's *in town* now. There's a new elementary school where our house once stood and the rest of the 40 acres is a fine new residential district."

In every western state we have heard stories that are substantially the same. They are true, unexaggerated stories; and they would lead one to believe that the only real suckers were the ones who had the chance to buy large parcels of cheap land in the paths of progress but who lacked the vision or the faith to do it.

Al Hartwig, like many real estate men we met in our journey, had both vision and faith. So did a number of just plain people who have listened to these men, and prospered accordingly. In fact, one might say axiomatically, that to be a successful pioneer one must have both vision and faith. Our definition of a successful pioneer is a person with enough faith to buy the land while it's cheap and enough fortitude to hold it until it isn't. After that he takes his profit and becomes a successful land investor.

Remember what we said, facetiously? "A good investment is a speculation on which you guessed right." It must be clear now that by following the simple rules in this book, you can do much to make your "guess" an informed one.

Earlier we said that in the process of looking for land you will meet a lot of nice people. It happens to us all of the time. For instance, just before we sat down to put together the material for this chapter we took another overnight trip to the Antelope Valley, which covers about 41 per cent of Los Angeles County and a good portion of East Kern County.

With Lou and Ann Tedesco, associates and friends from the New York television days and now neighbors of ours in Willow Springs, we were driving to see the excavation for a large, artificial water-skiing lake that had been started in the area. As we drove to the site, a car came opposite us and stopped. The driver, who introduced himself as Harry Long, president of a well-known oil and engineering company in Southern California, asked if we knew anything about the area.

We did—and we gladly imparted what we knew in an informal "running-board conference" which was followed up a few days later with another session in his office on Wilshire Blvd. in Los Angeles.

Most of the discussion centered around the growth possibilities in the Willow Springs area of the Antelope Valley and the need for additional recreational facilities in that whole Emerald Triangle area.

Later, after the main business had been discussed, we were looking north from his office window in the Lee Tower, which is Los Angeles' tallest office building at the moment. We happened to mention that we had photos of the same general area taken from 1900 through the present. The growth is unbelievable.

Mr. Long nodded. "My people came here from Colorado in 1912. You can imagine the changes we've seen!"

We could, partly from personal recollection and partly from the photographs, the scores of them, from which the illustrations in this book were chosen.

Mr. Long knew that we were interested in land investment

as an avocation. We discussed various localities in the West and called his attention to the remarkable story on strip cities which appeared in the September 18, 1961, issue of *U.S. News & World Report*. We agreed that 25 years ago it would have been difficult indeed to have forecast with any accuracy the actual (and incredible) growth of some of the areas. For instance, when a friend of ours, Gordon Jenkins, the brilliant conductor-composer, wrote the catchy "I'll Make The San Fernando Valley My Home" back in the early forties, none of us ever imagined, despite the song's tremendous popularity, that within twenty years the valley would actually become a solid sea of citizens. We travel it every day or so, struggle through its freeway traffic, and it is still hard to believe.

Harry Long told us that he bought 30 acres in the city of San Fernando at the extreme northwestern end of the valley in 1940. He thought it seemed a fair buy at $650 an acre. Today, the average value of that land is $25,000 an acre . . . and Mr. Long still owns it! There were a lot of struggling farmers out there when Mr. Long bought his land. If they have held, they are poor no more. They're probably on one of those cruise ships!

The reason we keep going over these real-life stories is simple: It is hard to believe that such wealth can actually happen to us because we had the good fortune to buy and hold a certain piece of land.

Not long ago the newspapers carried a story about actor Joel McCrea and the ranch he had been persuaded to buy when he was a young actor just starting toward stardom.

According to the report, Mr. McCrea sold 1000 acres of his ranch in nearby Ventura County to a subdivider for $3,000,000. The new owner plans to build several thousand private dwellings, some apartments, several schools, and a shopping center. (See how the megaloctopus reaches out?)

But Mr. McCrea still retains 650 acres (a shade better than a square mile!) of the property he originally purchased in

1933. The story goes on to say that Mr. McCrea had made a previous sale of 54 acres in 1959 from which he had realized $1,300,000. That would make nearly *four and one half million dollars realized* from only a portion of the original ranch . . . *in less than three decades!*

We wanted to know something of the circumstances surrounding Joel McCrea's original decision to invest his money in land instead of some of the other things that might have tempted him in 1933. So we wrote to him and very quickly received a most courteous and interesting letter, which reads in part:

Thank you for your letter. It is true that in 1931 while making a film with Will Rogers on location at Lake Tahoe I told him I was 24 years old now and I was going to save my money and buy a ranch.

Will Rogers said to me, "Don't wait until you have saved money enough to buy a ranch, buy one now and work to pay for it. I am sure you will make it. If you don't do it now you will probably end up spending your money and driving around Hollywood in a convertible winking at girls!"

I took his advice and after working for several years ran on to this place in Ventura County in 1933 and, as Will advised me, I purchased it with a down payment of $5000. As you no doubt have read in the papers, I have recently sold part of it and for a great deal more than I ever anticipated. I shall never forget Will Rogers, not only because he gave me such sound advice but because he was a fine American and a great friend . . .

Receiving that letter from Joel McCrea was a special pleasure. We feel that the things he said about Will Rogers may, in all justice, be said about Mr. McCrea too. How many wonderful hours of entertainment he's given us on the screen over the years!

What Will Rogers understood about the growth of the West and the value of its land is now being imparted to many other stars of screen and television who must find, in their high-earning years, the safest, most inflationproof investments for their dollars.

Shortly before his tragic death, we sat on the dock at Newport Harbor with Dick Powell, talking about land. Dick was still purchasing property. "The profits I made in early land investments are still buying real estate for me," he said. "A lot of people think this property has reached its peak," he added, indicating the once deserted sand bars that in less than a quarter of a century have become one of the most valuable concentrations of real estate in the world. "As high as it is, I think it's only beginning its increase!"

Dick backed up his judgment with hard cash. So far as we know he never missed on a piece of property he bought and held. Nor have many others. Some of the stars who have bought and held are: John Wayne, Richard Boone (who, along with others, owns not far from us in the Antelope Valley), Dana Andrews, Bing Crosby, Bob Hope, Fred MacMurray, Loretta Young, Dennis Weaver, Lloyd Bridges, Lloyd Nolan, and Don DeFore to name just a few. *Bonanza's* Lorne Greene has purchased in New Mexico and is reported to have built there a practical replica of the great log house, Ponderosa, which is his home in the television series.

Perhaps one of the reasons more of us so-called average people don't realize the opportunities in buying and holding good land is because we tend to say to ourselves, "Sure movie stars and millionaires can afford to buy the stuff and hold it. But what about those of us who have to get by on far less?"

Well—certainly it's not as easy. But it can be done. There are literally thousands of success stories in land investment—and most of them do involve the average wage earner type of investor who often had to scrounge to make the payments and keep the kids in shoes. If we tried to document just those stories we know to be true because they happened to friends and acquaintances, we could cover 10 acres with the manuscript alone!

Before we introduce you to two of the saddest characters we know, we'd like to tell you something that happened to us recently. Certainly everyone agrees that, as a group, schoolteachers are not overpaid. This little story involves some "worthless" city lots in Laguna Beach, California, a world famous art colony and seaside resort and our home for the past few years.

Two schoolteachers, now retired, who have asked us not to use their names, purchased five lots near us in 1943. The lots were in an unimproved subdivision. Streets were drawn on the subdivider's maps alright, but no one had bothered to cut them along the contours of the steep hills overlooking the beach. Finally, sometime later, one narrow street was scraped almost to the top of a nearby hill. It went within a hundred feet of the five lots. Four of the lots were 25 feet by 100 feet. The fifth lot was a pie-shaped piece of land measuring roughly 10,000 square feet. The two nice ladies paid $2750 for the five of them.

Today, just 21 years later, these two ladies politely turned down our offer of $30,000 for the lots. There is still no street, but there is one of the most magnificent coastline views in California. And they know it!

After paying interest for several years and taxes for two decades, these two schoolteachers could make a capital gains profit of well over $20,000. That's a tidy sum of keeping money. But they don't need it. You see, some years earlier they had also purchased some raw acreage in California's San Joaquin Valley.

"That land has made us a nice profit too, Mr. and Mrs. Cooley," they explained almost apologetically, "so we have enough money to meet our needs. And in the meantime we understand the values are still going up in Laguna." To that we can only add, "Are they ever!"

We haven't given up though. Our friend Ken Murray was quick to point out the mistake in our approach to these two ladies. "Next time you make those schoolteachers an offer, take along two big red apples!"

Now let's meet the two saddest characters in the country, Mr. I. Hadda and Mr. I. Coulda. These two gents live everywhere in the land and they may be heard weeping loudly every time some friend tells them about a land sale in the area that has turned a fine profit.

"I hadda chance to buy that land for $100 an acre a coupla years go!" you'll hear one of them cry. And his sad friend will immediately chime in, "I coulda bought the piece next to it for less than that!"

Here's a little story about Jim Jeffries. We "hadda" chance to buy 10 acres in North Hollywood in 1933 right next to the former heavyweight champion's famous "Barn." The price was $500 an acre and we "coulda" borrowed the money to do it. But there was a depression on and we owed several thousand dollars, including a whopping hospital bill. Total weekly income was $44.00. Land was the last thing in the world we seemed to need. And besides, the Barn was surrounded by vegetable fields on one side and sagebrush on the other and just beyond it "twisters" (small tornados) used to send columns of sand and dust several hundred feet in the air. The farmers blasted away at the never-ending horde of jack rabbits that raided their crops every sundown. It was not promising land . . . and the prospects for the country at large did not seem promising either, what with bank holidays and all.

So, despite Big Jim's earnest plea that we take the land, we begged off. He couldn't understand our lack of foresight and our unwillingness to gamble on a sure thing. By consulting that most dependable of all indices, hindsight, we can't understand our decision now either.

Jim is gone now and his famous Barn is a boxing museum at Knott's Berry Farm in Buena Park. Also gone are the jack rabbits and the vegetables they raided. But the land is still there . . . tucked under one of the most densely settled commercial sections in California.

When we asked around to try to determine the present value of the land we were told that it would probably have to be reckoned in square feet. That same 10 acres, which would have cost us $5000 on the easiest possible terms, today is worth somewhere around $1,250,000. One estimate nearly doubled that!

So, we, too, have had occasion to say "I hadda" and "I coulda"! But the beautiful part of it is, we no longer sing that sad refrain—not since Captain Ken Stein literally shanghaied us aboard his ferry boat and took us, shivering and miserable, to Fire Island Pines just a decade ago.

And when *people pressure* forces home seekers or business to spill over on our land in Stuart, Florida, and in Southern California's Antelope Valley, we'll sing no sad refrains, you can bet. We'll just do some thinking; we'll see if the offer makes sense; we'll see if we have a new place scouted in which to invest—in one of the dozen or more strip cities and islands in the country; then we'll make our decision, put another block in our own land pyramid, as L. McLean calls it, and we'll join those jolly farmers on another cruise! And when we do, we'll take time out to thank the Good Lord and the Ken Steins for having the thoughtfulness and persistence to keep after us until we did what every average wage earner should do "for his own good."

We don't say that everyone can do what we are presently doing. In fact, we couldn't in the beginning either—but for the last couple of years, *one half* of all money earned in our family goes into a special "land account." It lies there earning interest until we find something that looks like a good, raw land investment. We recently tapped the land account again, to buy a quarter section—160 acres—here in the West. There is a piece of land in New Mexico that we want too— and one in Arizona, along the path of the new Route 66; and some in Utah on Route 40, near a growing "island" of *people pressure;* and let's not forget wonderful chances in Colorado, Nevada, Oregon, and Washington too. We've seen it all!

Often we felt that our tax consultant was convinced we were land crazy—even dangerous—victims of some sort of strange new compulsion. But lo and behold! The other day he broached the subject—rather hesitantly—and wanted to know if we would help *him* locate some acreage for his own family. "You two seem to have the knack for getting land right smack in the path of progress," he said. We told him *anybody* can acquire that "knack" and with a lot less trouble than it took us, if they'll follow what we have had to say in this land primer and then dig into some of the more advanced books on the subject if they wish to enlarge their knowledge.

We told our friend to follow our blueprint. He replied, "We will, but the next time you go out, can the wife and I go with you?" You bet they can. And by the time they are able to buy this book, we'll also bet they are the proud owners of a piece of the Golden West. If you want to know what proud landowners look like, we suggest you look again at the candid photo we took of Lou and Ann Tedesco scooping up some western soil to put in a bottle on the mantel in their New York City apartment. They say it will comfort them until they can move West too.

12

HEADIN' FOR THE LAST ROUNDUP

For a few paragraphs let's do a little reviewing. It may help you to crystallize in your minds some of the very basic elements in this formula for finding your parcel of valuable western land.

Please remember, however, this book does *not* pretend to be a textbook or an advanced course in western raw land investment. *It is what it is*—a *first reader* or *primer* of western land values and the steps that can lead to successful investment in land *if you will follow them,* taking the trouble along the way to add to your knowledge all of the pertinent facts about the area in which you are interested.

We have tried to keep these pages from being dull. But in keeping them lively and informal we realize that we run the risk of having some folks feel that because the book isn't full of scholarly language and columns of facts and figures that it is not authoritative. To that we would say, "There is nothing in this book that has not been confirmed by personal experience, by personal research, or by recognized authorities in the areas covered."

Facts and figures will change under the influence of the tremendous force we call *people pressure*. Western growth is so rapid now that up-to-date figures are out of date almost before they can be compiled, printed, and distributed to the public.

But the basic principles of sound investigation and research *before* you buy will never be out of date. In fact it is fair to say that they will become more and more timely as the years go by.

This short review, then, will be concerned with those basic and unchanging principles that do not become dated.

We'll throw caution to the winds again and "assume" that you've gotten this far in the book because the subject matter interests you. You are "hooked," or you are about to be, on your own personal piece of western land.

We have taken the pains to tell you a number of true stories in these pages, stories of men and the fortunes they have made by buying and holding well-placed western land.

It is true that not all of them understood the principles involved in "How to Get Squeezed by a Megaloctopus." Many of them simply loved the West, moved into its heaviest population centers, bought land in or around such places, and had the good luck or foresight to hold on to it.

We have traced the amazing history of the growth of our country from the first harbors along the East Coast to the fantastic strip cities described in Chapter Five. We have shown that people pressure, exerted along the transportation lines of least resistance, has resulted in great ribbons of urban and suburban development that have all but saturated thirteen basic areas of our country. We have shown you "islands" of people pressure that perhaps, in the not too distant decades, will actually spread out and merge with the strip city nearest to it. Las Vegas, Nevada, seems to give promise of that. Reno, Sparks, and Carson City and the Lake Tahoe complex seem also to give promise of doing that, of merging eventually with the Stockton–Sacramento–San Francisco strip city. There are several others, as you have seen on the strip city map. Our "Megaloctopus" is no respecter of state lines.

In showing you the pattern of this growth we have also shown you the areas in which there are fine, raw land investment potentials. We have also shown you how to question yourself as to the sort of investment you wish to make in land —and for whom—yourselves, your children, your grandchildren?

We have shown by example what happened to our "jolly farmers" who sweated and struggled for years to eke out a living until they finally discovered that their land was caught in the benevolent squeeze of our "Megaloctopus."

Incidentally, while on a brief follow-up research trip for this book, we stopped in to look at a fine new cooperative apartment complex growing up on the cliffs overlooking Newport Beach and Balboa here in Southern California's booming Orange County.

The sales representative was a real old-timer, Ole Hanson, Jr., whose father was one of California's pioneer land developers. (He founded the City of San Clemente.) Mr. Hanson told us the story of a fine Italian lady, the widow of a prominent farmer in the area, who had recently sold out the family's pinto-bean and soy-bean fields for many thousands of dollars an acre. The lady wished to invest the money again, "in something solid." So she came to the elegant new development, practically on the edge of her old property, and began negotiations for *eight* of the residences. If the purchase goes through, it will total better than a quarter of a million dollars!

It will be a fine commission for Mr. Hanson, Jr., who by the

the way doesn't need it, because for many years he has been holding cattle-ranch acreage down the coast from Newport, in the hills back of the city his father founded.

"It may seem kind of silly to be running Hereford and Black Angus cattle on $10,000 an acre pasture . . . but that's what it's come to!" he said. "I'm *in* the real estate business, but I didn't think it would happen *this* fast."

Of one thing we are certain after our visit with Ole Hanson, Jr.; his sons will have a terrific legacy. "I'm building up this land estate for them," Mr. Hanson said. "I can still get up on my horse and cut out a steer or a calf, but it's their turn next," he added. "I've had a wonderful life, putting our place together."

From the hearty laugh and the smile crinkles at the corners of his eyes, we are inclined to agree—Mr. Hanson has had a wonderful life, indeed! And he is the first to say, "Thanks to western land!"

We didn't ask Mr. Hanson how much he paid for the considerable acreage he holds in the hills back of San Clemente (enough to run 200 head of cattle) but we know that only 25 years ago that land was selling for less than $500 an acre. It was Mr. Hanson who called it "$10,000 an acre pasture" now. From our own attempts to make modest purchases of such land we know that $10,000 an acre for that land on the near ocean side of the hills is very conservative.

Farmers, small businessmen, widows, average people are the owners, or were the owners, of that land. They "just happened" to be in a *people pressure* area.

And what we've said to you is this: You, too, can find a piece of land that will eventually lie in a people pressure area—if you will follow the simple set of rules or guides set down in these pages.

You know the anatomy of a megalopolis now—a strip city —and how it grows. And you know one of the ways of predicting where it will most likely develop . . . along the new highways and freeways that connect the principal population centers in the region.

We have told you how to scout your home town or home city area and, by comparing old maps and watching the papers and magazines for stories of new freeways being planned, how to focus your search down to a specific area. And then, by utilizing the expert help of the brokers and realtors in the area, we have shown you how to zero in on your own particular piece of western land.

By asking the thirteen questions posed by the National Better Business Bureau and reproduced with their permission in Chapter Eight, we have shown you how to protect yourself against misrepresentation or unfortunate omissions of valuable facts.

We have said that it is imperative to enlist the services of a good title insurance company to confirm and insure the validity of your title to the land.

In the case of western land this title insurance is an absolute necessity. The modest fees these companies charge are miniscule when compared to the service and peace of mind they provide by searching the title of the land you wish to purchase, back to its very beginnings; by making certain there are no tax liens or other encumbrances on the land; by issuing an insurance policy which holds you harmless from loss in case there is some question about clear title.

These title insurance companies are remarkable institutions. One of them, Title Insurance and Trust Company in Los Angeles, is not only an indispensable adjunct to orderly growth in the state but it is also a remarkable private museum of historical data. It was from their fascinating collection that most of the old photographs came. There are a number of fine title insurance companies in the West, and if you buy land you should insist upon using the services of one of them. No chance then for another Limantour swindle! Actually, today there is little chance of such an ingenious con game. But titles can be clouded in many ways, simply because the sale and recording of land is a complicated procedure and it is done by human beings who make honest errors. It is the function of the title companies to protect you against those errors, if and when they happen. They do that, admirably.

The thirteen "safe-guides" as we call the Better Business Bureau's questions cover most of the possible areas of misunderstanding and misrepresentation. But in Chapter Nine, "The Anatomy of a Murderous Investment," we have shown you some of the techniques used by those who would deliberately mislead you. Often, as we said, this is done to "lure" you to a place so the promoter can show you what a really good deal he has. This has been called a "questionable" advertising practice. And we feel it is, really. But let's say once again that it is not only the land developers who use such tactics. Most competitive selling today is filled with extravagant language psychologically designed to induce, seduce, or frighten you into buying. Everything from snob appeal to sob appeal is used.

We know! We were once a part of a small group of "creative" New York advertising people who loosed upon this land such spot campaigns as BEEEEEE-OOOOOOOH, which got people sudsy in places never reached by ordinary soaps . . . and another little gem, the destroyer whistle that went WHOOOOOOP-WHOOOOOOP-WHOOOOOOP! and sent millions of smokers rushing pell-mell to the nearest tobacco counter. There were a lot more, too, including one that was finally banned by the New York City Board of Education for disrupting music classes. That little beauty involved a wine and was commercial subversion of the lowest order. But it *was* clever.

Advertising men *are* clever . . . and creative . . . and relentless in their fight for their client's share of the market. Whether you agree or not (the novel, *The Hucksters*, actually did them a grave injustice) they are a vital component in the sales machine that makes America's economy run smoothly. Their role has changed from passive to active salesman . . . and they are both vanguard and backstop for the salesman in the field. The reputable ones—and that is by far the great majority—are enthusiastic, yes, but not reckless. Most of the abuses in land advertising recently may be laid at the door of small "house" agencies who are under the domination of the selling company. But once again, the thirteen "safe-guides," those land shark-repellent questions suggested by the Better Business Bureau, are your best first line of defense against being carried away by a lot of illusive, allusive adjectives that create mouth-watering mirages in western desert land. Modern realtors put it this way; "INVESTIGATE BEFORE YOU INVEST!" In the days of the Roman Empire, the ethical brokers put it this way, "CAVEAT EMPTOR! —[Let the Buyer Beware!]"

13

INTO THE FUTURE VIA THE PAST

When the late Hollywood columnist and Doubleday authoress, Hedda Hopper, drove from her home to the city of Anaheim in Orange County, California, to autograph her best-seller, *The Whole Truth and Nothing But,* she was so flabbergasted by the changes that she was moved to comment in her column:

"It seems but a few years ago that I used to motor through the sleepy little village of Anaheim and nearly swoon from the fragrance of orange groves lining the road on either side. When I went down recently to sign some books I couldn't believe my eyes. Crisscrossed with freeways, aswarm with housing developments, Anaheim is a big city!"

Hedda Hopper's reaction was not unusual, neither did it mean that she was any the less aware of the growth in the West than anyone else. On the contrary, it simply meant that she, like most of us unless we have deliberately moved back for a look as we've had to do to write this book, are so close to the people we can't see the progress.

Since 1855 there have been five major land booms in the West. The second came in 1875, the third in 1887 with the coming of the railroads and the violent competition between the Southern Pacific and the Santa Fe lines. The fourth came in 1923 when Southern California had its famous "Bastard Spanish" boom and the fifth began after World War II in 1946. Like a juggernaut it continues to roll onward and there seems to be no end to it. For this time it is the result of people pressure on a nation-wide scale, in fact on a world-wide scale. This time the cry of living room is no mere political expedient as it was in the days of Hitler and Mussolini in the 1930s and 1940s. This time, with our own population heading for the 330 million mark by the year A.D. 2000, we are indeed in danger of running out of living room and a lot of other things too.

Living room means only one thing . . . *land.*

After another brief look at the history of western migration in this past century we're going to pass on to you a prediction made by a respected research organization that will, in all probability, leave you as incredulous as we were when it first came to our attention.

But to take the best possible measure of tomorrow, let's look again at yesterday.

In Chapter Five we saw how the population pattern began to grow from the East and how, in the early 1800s, it began to make its first contact with the Spanish settlements in Alta, California, "alta" because it lay north of, or above, Baja or lower California.

First under Spanish and then under Mexican rule, the Californios—and many were Americans who had given up their citizenship in return for Mexican land grants—were living an idyllic life until the first Yankee traders put into San Diego, Dana Point, and Monterey.

Then came the overland expeditions—largely military-political explorations like that of John C. Frémont, adventurous son-in-law of expansionist, Senator Thomas Hart Benton of Missouri.

On January 13, 1847, one year before the discovery of gold at Sutter's Mill, Frémont accepted the surrender of General Andrés Pico and signed the Treaty of Cahuenga (across the street from the present Universal-International studios), which ended the war with Mexico in California and effectively brought the territory under American domination.

Gold! January 24, 1848! On that fateful morning when John Marshall's eye caught the glint of the first gold in the mill race, there were only about ten thousand so-called "whites" in the California territory. Two years later, 1850, when California was admitted to the Union, the population had grown to almost a quarter of a million!

It was inevitable that, when the first boom excitement had passed and the more stable "settler element" began taking up land, many of the disillusioned would remember places they had passed through on their way to the diggings. Numbers of them, after looking at the political and economic confusion engendered by the occupation and the gold rush, turned eastward again and took up land in the territories that would later become Nevada, Arizona, New Mexico, Idaho, Colorado, and Utah. The settling of the West had begun. In the hundred years that have followed, the process has never stopped. In fact it has hardly even slowed down except for the brief slumps in immigration that inevitably follow each so-called "boom" peak.

Isolated from the Union as it was, the new state of California became a prime incentive for the United States to consolidate all of the vast intervening western territory that now makes up the eleven (actually thirteen) western states. Consolidation meant expedition; expedition meant new routes, which meant immigration, settlement, and expansion—simply the primary and secondary phases of the pattern of growth that eventually led to the development of the modern strip city or megalopolis. The process has never changed, except in degree.

Because the history of those early years is so filled with adventure (they were the years in which our western legendry was born) we are tempted to expand this book for the sheer excitement of retelling some of the tales. But we'll resist the temptation and suggest that by way of heightening your own interest in the piece of the West you own, or wish to own, you yourself dig into one of the hundred or more wonderful books covering the history of the West. We know of no more absorbing reading. There are two other rewards also: First, your piece of the West will become a part of living history which is just now entering its most fabulous stage; Second, *it is impossible to enter into the spirit of this great country of ours through the pages of its history without becoming rededicated to the principles set down for its preservation by our Founding Fathers.* Does any American need a better reason for knowing his land?

Let's move ahead to the present, which is becoming the past even as this is being written. It is useless to attempt to set down the current state of western growth in the pages of a book that needs six to nine months to be manufactured. By the time the first copy could get off the presses the facts and figures, as such, would be out of date.

So let's not attempt to "freeze" any figures which might for a fleeting moment be accurate measures of our present growth. Read your newspapers and news magazines and do it faithfully. You'll get a moving, up to the minute measure of our progress that cannot be bettered. Radio and television public service shows are vital too.

Mark and tear out those articles that can become useful

evidence of growth in the area you're interested in. Start a land file. Once you begin it, you'll be amazed at how many stories bear directly on some aspect of the growth patterns of the area in which you own or in which you are about to own. Once a month, leaf back through your file and weed out the stories that have been superceded by later information. If you keep it all (as we do for purposes of comparison) it will soon crowd you out of your own quarters. The photo of a small part of our research, in this book, proves it!

If you are somewhere around thirty years old in the publication year of this book (1964) you will be just about reaching retirement age in the year A.D. 2000 . . . the "turn of the century!"

Most of the research that is being done now, on which our country's future needs are being based, is projected to the year 2000. The year 2000 has an H. G. Wellsian sound, doesn't it? (Let's hope some of his predictions don't come true!)

Projecting the probable future of the west by mentally equating it with the probable future of America, as our researchers see it, the first stunning prediction is this:

By the year 2000, we will lack 50,000,000—*fifty million*—acres of land for our needs—*even if we have used up every available acre of desert, swamp, and mountain top!*

Now even though you are tempted to toss this book out of the window as the work of a pair of daffy land addicts, don't do it. *We didn't make up those figures!* They were issued in March of 1963 by a private research firm called Resources for the Future Inc., in Washington, D.C.; and the press reported that much of its financial support came from the august Ford Foundation.

Now we must confess that we can't quite grasp that picture either. We keep thinking of the vast stretches of vacant land—often a hundred miles or more in length—along Nevada's highways in which we saw not a single human being.

There are similar stretches in Arizona, New Mexico, and in most of the other western states. There are some sizable desert stretches in southeastern California too.

They said it, we didn't—all that land is going to be needed —and 50 million acres more!

We can't make more land; so what are we going to do?

We don't suppose those researchers are suggesting that we will have to resort to something as controversial as birth control, infanticide, or mass annihilation. Despite the fact that everybody knows that one tragic goof in Washington or Moscow would make the land problem academic, nobody is suggesting that killing people or stopping their creation is the answer here.

What the researchers are searching for are not just visionary pictures of the future but ways and means of coping with it. Certainly a fifty million-acre land shortage is an emergency of the first magnitude. The solution they seek then must be in methods of utilizing more efficiently our one fixed asset, land.

It must be obvious, too, that the law of supply and demand will be more sharply and widely operative in the land market than in any other. The research of all of the groups probing into our future and its problems seems to bear this out. If we are land short, then automatically, in some areas, we are water short—we are mineral short and we are timber short— or by the year 2000 we will be.

Some of these conditions appear to exist already. Many areas in the West are water short at present. Hopefully, for the immediate future, relieving that water shortage is largely a matter of transporting water from areas where there is a surplus. Plans are under way in the West for doing that now. The famous Feather River Project in California is one such endeavor. Many others are on the rough planning boards of state and federal water-resources groups and are being considered in the long-range planning of such huge semipublic utilities as Los Angeles' Metropolitan Water District, the largest such organization (wholesale water distributors) in the world—and the one with the most difficult continuing problem.

Plans being considered now envision bringing water to desert areas in the West from California's Eel River and Trinity River in the largely untapped Coast Range Watershed. Also, a furor is in the making over a proposal to bring water south from the Snake River in Idaho. De-salting sea water already has a good start at the pilot plant in San Diego. Other plants are planned. And one fantastic plan calls for damming the Straits of Carquinez in upper San Francisco Bay to impound the hundreds of millions of acre feet of unused water that now flow into the sea from the Sacramento and San Joaquin rivers and their tributaries. That has been a dream since the turn of this century. It has been laughed at, scoffed at, called impractical and even idiotic. But we may have to come to it yet. One engineer we lunched with not long ago said that with full use of all of our untapped California and Oregon water resources, we would be able to meet the needs of our own growth and that of Nevada and Arizona too. Another engineer said, "Hooey!" or words to that effect.

But one thing everyone agrees on; we're going to have to start taking mighty good care of *all* of our resources from now on—and it's a lot later than we think!

It is true that from time to time we read reassuring reports that our water and our coal and our oil and timber reserves are sufficient for our needs in the foreseeable future. But what no one has accurately foreseen until now (if the latest research is anywhere near correct) is the rapid acceleration of our population growth and the resultant increase in *people pressure*.

People pressure doesn't mean just a decrease in elbow

room. It also means an *increase* in consumption of the basic needs of our way of life. The primary needs of course are food, drink, and clothing, although in the case of the latter some of the fabrics may be made out of thin air. In fact, if you go to the beach these days and see what some of our cute young things are wearing, you suspect that they are making some of those bikinis out of thin air now.

But back to the future! (How's *that* again?) We'll admit you have to look and listen closely to even begin to grasp what apparently is in store for Americans who will be here to celebrate the advent of the twenty-first century—which event is only 36 years away.

Take a look at some of the figures projected for the year 2000:

We now have 200 million people in the United States (as of September 1967).

We *will* have 350 million by the year 2000.

We now have 60 million autos in use.

We *will* have 250 million in use by the year 2000.

We now build 1.7 million new homes a year.

We *will* build 5 million new homes a year by the year 2000.

We now have a labor force of 73 million persons.

We *will* have a labor force of 142 million by the year 2000.

. . . and so it goes, new figures rendering yesterday's figures obsolete before the ink is dry. All of the comforting reports about having enough of most things to see us through the foreseeable future somehow do not sound so comforting in the light of a population that will double in the next 36 years—of a country that will be shy 50 million acres of needed land—based, of course, on present usage increases.

We could go on with figures until you were decimal daffy. But the simple point that should emerge from this welter of predicting and projecting and supposing is: What this country needs most is a good five-cent crystal ball—and what its nonland-owning citizens need most is to own a piece of land—and to hold it and pass it on to the next generation.

But let us say again right here: *We are not suggesting that, upon reading these projections, you rush right out and buy the first piece of vacant land you come across, at the asking price, without regard to your ability to pay for it or the suitability of the land for your present or future use.*

Despite the apparent sense of urgency about the national problem, we urge you to make haste *slowly* with your problem. Planners need decades to prepare for national economic emergencies. And even then we sometimes get the feeling they could have used still more time.

Never before has the world been faced with problems of such magnitude and complication as now. Each of us helps to cope with our country's problems and see them through to proper solutions by doing his share as a sober-minded, responsible citizen. The place to start is at home, with sober-minded decisions about your family's future. The future of each family in the land *is* the future of the land. Its people *are* the "spirit in the land."

It would be well to recall the counsel of former Secretary of Commerce Luther Hodges, who urged every young American to invest in something of value that he can afford—to obligate himself to pay for it—but not beyond his ability to pay.

You can buy good land, at fair prices, for less money than you will have to pay for a new car. If you think you can't afford them both (and you surely need them both) then buy a compact car and a compact piece of land. You'll never miss a few inches of tail fin or wheel base . . . or for that matter a few horses under the hood. But one day you might miss a few square feet of land—more than you'll ever know!

The "things" we have bought—necessities all—have all depreciated; the land we have bought—a luxury we thought at first—has all increased in value. Much of it has doubled in cash worth—many times! *That*, we assure you, is the wonderful feeling often referred to as "security"!

14

PROMOTERS ARE PEOPLE

In fact, promoters are people who combine the financial know-how of an international banker with the flair of the showman and the conviction of the salesman. As we said in the second chapter, they are a colorful lot and occasionally they are controversial figures. The incidence of borderline operators among them is probably no higher than in any other high-pressure profession. By now we have met dozens of them in as many states. If you are interested in investing in western land and you have not already met some of these men or their representatives you most certainly will before long. Aside from their passionate belief in land and their talent for getting things done these men have little in common. The most successful of them range from a college professor with a doctor's degree in sociology to a former sharecropper who dropped off a freight train in the early thirties. With no education beyond a keen ability to size up his fellow men he has become a multimillionaire.

Because of the flurry of attention in the press in recent months a lot of people think the big land developer or promoter is a fairly recent phenomenon. Actually he has been with us since the first colony was founded at Jamestown. In Europe and in the Orient he has been around a lot longer than that.

A land promoter may not necessarily be one who packages and sells land. He may be simply one who is enthusiastic about a certain area or areas and who has the means to let large numbers of people know about it. (On that basis, the authors might qualify!) Both General John C. Frémont and Mark Twain were vitally instrumental in promoting the value of California land in their writings. Much of Twain's *Roughing It* and Frémont's *Narratives of Exploration and Adventure* read like land promoters' commercials of the most extravagant nature. And these men actually influenced a lot of people to immigrate. The present-day land promoter's pitches are not couched in such polished prose, but they certainly induce in a lot of people the desire to immigrate. The fine brochures produced by development boards, progress associations, action committees, and chambers of commerce may be said to be land promotions in a very direct sense. And the United States Government itself, through its land offices, is one of the world's largest and most aggressive land promoters. Some of the advertising copy it uses to accomplish its purposes could hardly be called a literal statement of the fact, as more than one indignant private land promoter is quick to point out when under fire.

Be that as it may, land promoters have always been with us and always will be. And because they are mortals and subject to mortal frailties some of them will incur official displeasure. In this world things are never all good or all bad. As we read through the reams of studies and reports made available to us one clear point continues to emerge: The official problem of defining land investment as opposed to land speculation is, as one researcher puts it, "as complicated as unscrambling eggs!"

In Part One of "The Unanchored Subdivision," a report on the economic problems of promotional subdivisions prepared by the Graduate School of Business Administration of the University of California at Los Angeles, Edward Elias, Jr., co-author of the complete report, defines land value as deriving from "the stream of income or services which a parcel of land is able to return to its owner."

We think that is the best definition of land value we have seen. Unfortunately for those who are trying to work out practical legal restraints on unethical subdividers this basic definition applies equally well to the value placed on land by the seller and the buyer.

A promoter who sees a 60 per cent net profit in a vast area of remote desert land after he has scuffed unimproved ranch roads through it will see great dollar value in the sun-baked wasteland. Once peddled it might "serve" to make him millions.

On the other hand, many a customer who unwittingly falls for his extravagant, if not downright misleading, pitches may find absolutely no dollar value whatever in his 2½-acre ranchito in his own lifetime. If dollar value were the only criterion by which to judge the service a piece of land renders to its owner then it is safe enough to say that most investors in remote desert subdivisions have wasted their money.

But what about those people—postman Al Cook among them—who are actually happy to be living in the wide-open spaces often under conditions as primitive as any encountered by the covered-wagon pioneers?

"Folks, if you had come from a cold-water flat in Brooklyn, this would look like paradise to you!" Remember that statement? Certainly that man's dehydrated patch of paradise is rendering a service to its owner. No wonder the dictionary uses half a column to define the word, value.

Again: *The important thing is to make up your mind why, and for whom you are buying the land. Having done that, ask those thirteen questions—and insist on straight answers.*

If you have truthfully answered the first self-imposed questions, then you have bought a piece of land that fits your specifications; you have made a good investment and the value received by both you and the seller is "fair, just and equitable."

Of course, if you swear that you are happy with your purchase simply because you don't want to admit that you were taken, then that is a matter between you and your conscience —and, quite probably, your "better half."

Once in a while authors are fortunate enough to stumble on research that turns out to be living history directly related to their subject matter. Not long ago that happened to us.

While visiting with former theatrical associates and now fellow "Lagunatics" Barbara and Harvey Stephens, we began talking about old family documents.

After a few moments, Harvey, a highly respected actor who often graces your television screen, disappeared and returned with an old, metal strongbox. In it were a number of papers which had belonged to his grandfather, John Henry Stephens, a pioneer settler in San Bernardino, California, in the 1870s.

The document that interested us most was an 82-page handwritten letter sent by Grandfather Stephens to his good friend back in Wisconsin, one Homer D. L. Sweet. It took us two hours to read the fine Spencerian script. Time had dimmed the ink but not the incredible story the letter told. Its chief interest for us, however, is the insight it gives us concerning the practices of the promoters in the great land-boom days of the 1880s.

The letter is dated June 7, 1883, slightly before the bitter rivalry broke out between the two railroads that resulted in transporting settlers to California from as far away as Chicago for a total fare of one dollar each!

Here is a portion of Grandfather Stephens' account of his first venture in real estate. We should preface it by saying that over the years he went on to amass a fortune in it!

Speaking of his wife and himself, he writes, "Mary has done much, very much, toward carrying us through our financial struggles and has purchased with her own earnings [as a schoolteacher] a tract of five acres in a growing town which is now reckoned to be worth a thousand dollars.

"Yesterday, with Mary's buggy and Henry's [their son's] horse, Mary and I rode over to the new settlement, or colony, some 12 miles from here, which was commenced I think within 2 years—where we went last July, and where she purchased a half-lot, five acres. We found a large portion of the settlement being graded and improved otherwise.

"No fences are to be seen as each settler needs to keep his own stock out of mischief. For miles we could see orchards of oranges, apricots, peaches, nectarines, and vineyards almost without number, all or nearly all of which have been set out within the last year and all wearing the healthiest green imaginable. Not a leaf killed by last winter's frost!

"The land is laid out in ten acre tracts, though one half and sometimes even one quarter lots [2½ acres] are sold. And to the highest corner of every lot sold, an ample supply of water is carried in cement pipes and delivered in a hydrant, gauged to the exact quantity to which it is entitled.

"Springs have been searched out and tapped, dams built in the canyons, reservoirs made, pipes put in below the surface, and water furnished in abundance to land that without water produced nothing, but the water produced such growths of fruits and vegetables as astonished those who come here from beyond the mountains. [He refers to the midwest and east.]

"Having sold as much land as their stock of water would supply, the proprietors [promoters] suspended selling and commenced a search for more water. Some thirty miles away in an elevated valley they found a branch of our Santa Ana River where by building a dam they can make a lake and turning the stream before it reaches the Santa Ana, can bring the water to this settlement, or colony or town which they have named Redlands.

"So, soon the sale of the land will be resumed, and within the next six or seven years it is safe to predict that Redlands will contain thousands of inhabitants, a thriving, prosperous business, schools and churches, and such dense forests of deciduous and evergreen trees, fruit and ornamental trees, interspersed with vineyards, that a New Yorker, who had never been here nor learned of the marvels of the country—if brought here in the dark and set down blindfolded, would, when permitted to see, declare it had been in existence for half a century!"

(Authors' note: It is not surprising that Grandfather Stephens became a land promoter, is it?)

After some pages about his own plans, John Henry Stephens gets back to subdivisions again. He questions his friend:

"You have heard of Riverside? Well, it is about the same distance [12 miles] from here [San Bernardino]. Seven years ago in 1875 a small settlement was there—a post office and a school house. It was owned by a company which was selling land and digging ditches to bring water from the Santa Ana River.

"The president of that company took me over the land, miles and miles away—lands which seemed incapable of keeping rabbits alive, and made predictions which made me question his sanity.

"Well, that ground now, all over those many square miles that we rode that day, seven years ago, presents such a spectacle to a stranger as I have predicted for Redlands! No description within my scope of English would do it justice. That colony has applied for and is about to receive a city charter. I can name four or five such colonies within twenty miles that have commenced within a short period of time that promise as well as Redlands and Riverside."

Well there it is—a look at land and land promoters' operations back through time—back through eight decades—seen through the pages of pioneer John Henry Stephens' remarkable letter.

If you were to leaf through the advertisements used by those old land promoters you'd find the same "extravagant" adjectives, the same "outlandish" claims being used today. And still we know now that in the face of what actually happened, even their most extravagant claims became ultra-conservative. But many of those early promoters were called "crooks" by their contemporaries. Some of them were. There are crooks in almost every field of endeavor. The point is that the ones who built the lasting communities that are now important elements in the sprawling megalopolises of the nation appeared to some persons, at the time of their operations, to be just as overboard in their claims as many of the promoters who are packaging and peddling land today. And who is to say that within a very few decades from now, before our youngsters are grandparents, those once remote parts of "West Hellangone" won't also be verdant communities well within a megalopolis? Personally we wouldn't bet against it—not after studying Grandfather Stephens' lesson in history!

In addition to the other qualities we mentioned earlier it takes a special brand of vision and courage for a man to tear into a few thousand acres of virgin desert or mountain terrain and reshape it into a community. Often it takes an equal

amount of both to step into a community that isn't making it
and fix it up so it will.

For every land developer or promoter who uses questionable or downright dishonest methods of improving and selling there are a hundred land men who risk their credit and
their good health to do the job properly.

Among contemporary land developers the one who is
generally conceded to be the "dean of the raw land promoters" is a dynamic seventy-seven-year-old, cigar-chomping
bundle of perpetual optimism named M. Penn Phillips, one
of the most colorful figures in this controversial business.
His story is, in many respects, the story of Western land promotion and development in the past five decades.

Phillips was a child in Oklahoma when the last of the big
operators in the 1880s land boom were still casting their
magic spells on customers. In 1922 he came to California
and like many another before him he suddenly saw a vision
of the millions of people who would become the new wave
of western immigrants. Remembering lessons learned in the
southwest, Penn Phillips determined to divert some of their
dollars into his own developments. He chose Clear Lake,
California, for his first promotion.

Buying up land for a fraction of its potential worth, Phillips
measured out 10,000 lots in 1922, planted hundreds of trees,
built a hotel and a club. The growing population of San
Francisco, Oakland, and Berkeley responded to his vacation
land and gobbled up the parcels at an average price of $800
each. Today the choicest of those lots will bring ten times
that—*if* they come on the market.

After several more enterprises, Penn Phillips moved into
Coos Bay, Oregon. There he bought up thousands of tax sale
lots at one dollar each, fixed them up and sold them at three
for one hundred dollars. We asked him what he thought an
acre of that same water-front property would bring now.

"Around $25,000, I would say," he replied.

During our visit, Penn Phillips, displaying his phenomenal physical energy and youthful enthusiasm, showed us advance plans and maps of at least three developments scheduled for the near future. Among them was a seven thousand eight hundred acre Colorado River vacation development on land leased for sixty-five years from the Colorado River Indians under supervision of the Department of the Interior and the County of San Bernardino. It lies on the California side of the river. The half acre recreation sites run from $2000 to $8000 each with an annual land rental (lease fee) averaging $100 per year.

In addition to this Phillips development, his firm is acting as sales agent for the remarkable Green Tree community near Victorville, California and for Alta Sierra, an all-year residential and vacation community in the foothills of Northern California's Sierra Nevada.

Long gone are the old time "pitches" of the land promoter. "Every one of my salesmen tells the same story now," he said, "and there is no exaggeration—just facts."

This is achieved by the use of carefully produced sound-and-picture presentations projected for the customer right in his own home.

"We start the show and the prospect just sits there looking and listening for fifteen minutes. After that he either buys or not. He's got *all* the facts," says Phillips.

A lot of them buy—sight unseen, except for shadows on a "silver screen."

If M. Penn Phillips is the *alpha* of the land developers then Robert P. McCulloch is the *omega*. Or perhaps it would be more accurate to say that Mr. McCulloch is the precursor of a new generation of developer.

A distinguished industrialist, Chairman of the Board of the $40 million McCulloch Oil Corporation of California, his McCullough Properties subsidiary is building a major community, Lake Havasu City, on a 16,520 acre site on the Ari-

zona side of the Colorado River approximately midway
between Parker and Needles. The prestigious *Christian Science
Monitor* is quoted as saying, ". . . *one of the most am-
bitious projects ever attempted in the realm of private land
development.*"

Today Lake Havasu City can boast of all the usual metropolitan amenities plus some not often found at a new city's
doorstep—in this case the all-year recreational advantages
of the Colorado River.

Unlike most communities that only hope to attract industry, Lake Havasu City started with industry, installations
of the world-wide McCulloch manufacturing empire. Three
such plants are presently in operation turning out chain saws
and highly sophisticated heat treating, coil and carburetor
assembly production and stamping operations. There is also
a facility for testing the famed McCulloch outboard motors,
the need for which attracted Robert McCulloch to Lake
Havasu in the first place.

McCulloch Properties even operates its own regularly
scheduled passenger airline using a fleet of Lockheed Con-
stellations based in Chicago, Seattle, and Long Beach, California. Dozens of way-point communities are also served by
the FAA certified transports and crews. A major service and
maintenance hangar facility is located at the Long Beach
Airport.

So impressive are the Lake Havasu City accomplishments,
and so persuasive are its attractions, that approximately half
of the families who decide to fly there decide to buy there.
As of the beginning of 1967 investments in Lake Havasu
City were close to $25 million. Many professional observers
predict that Lake Havasu City will shortly rival both Phoenix
and Palm Springs as a prime winter resort; and because of
its solid all-year industrial base it is expected to easily out-
distance the latter.

McCulloch led the way and other giant corporations followed. In July 1967 the huge Atlantic Richfield Company, through its Western Properties Division, announced the purchase of an important property on Hawaii's island of Maui. In a joint development venture the huge refiner and marketer will build fee simple condominium residences with Blackfield Enterprises of Honolulu.

One of the most impressive developments to be undertaken is Rancho California midway between Los Angeles and San Diego. The owners of Rancho California, subsidiaries of Macco Realty Company (wholly owned by the Pennsylvania Railroad), Kaiser Aluminum & Chemical Corporation and Kaiser Industries Corporation, are presently implementing an extensive Master Plan which encompasses the entire 87,500 acre site—an area three times larger than the City of San Francisco.

If such a vast area can be called a "microcosm" then it is fair to say that, when realized, the plans will turn Rancho California into a microcosmic sample of the California macrocosm. In addition to miles of beautifully paved roads and streets, shopping centers, industrial sites, home sites, recreational facilities of every sort (the country's largest privately owned dam impounds 550 surface-acre Lake Vail, a hunter-fisherman's paradise), there are horse ranches, training facilities, commercial dairies, cattle ranches, farming and orchard units, all supplied with ample water, power and telephone facilities. The magnitude of the plan is staggering. It is definitely not for small speculators. It is for solid investors. Among others, Atlantic Richfield has bought 2000 acres here also. The day we visited the Rancho, Mrs. Elizabeth Whitney Tibbetts, owner of the famed racehorse Pretense, flew in by helicopter to take title to a 300-acre parcel. We were told that Mrs. Tibbetts was considering closing her facilities in the East and removing her training and breeding operations to Rancho California.

The "average investment" at Rancho California is said to

be "in the neighborhood of $60,000." Investments such as Mrs. Tibbetts' horse breeding and training facility could easily run in excess of a million dollars. The same may be said of the major vineyard and the larger citrus and avocado groves now being planted in the area. Rancho California is the largest of many holdings that once comprised the historic Vail Ranch.

"Promoters are people," we say, in captioning this chapter. But often now, as we have seen, promoters are also corporations, diversified corporations creating major land development subsidiaries as another highly profitable string to their corporate bows. Their huge financial resources may make for formidable competition. But individual enterprise can and still does pay off both for the developer and the investor. A prime example would be Incline Village on the north shore of Nevada's portion of Lake Tahoe in the High Sierra Nevada.

The financial wizard and master planner of this 9000 acre all-year residential and sports community is Arthur L. Wood, a former CPA from Oklahoma City. A highly successful venture in business property in Honolulu started Art Wood in the land developing profession. Surrounding himself with an imaginative and aggressive team, he has created one of the most exciting development miracles in the country.

One of Art Wood's primary concerns was to make the best possible use of the land; and that did not mean whacking it up into the greatest number of parcels. Far from it! Mr. Wood's purpose was to build an all-year residential and vacation community without destroying the natural beauty of the high mountain area. He and his planners have succeeded so well that five hundred homes built or building, schools, a city-size shopping center, churches, multimillion-dollar condominium residential projects such as U.S. Plywood's Crystal Shores and Rod Campbell's, The Cedars, are virtually "lost" in the virgin pine forest that surrounds the north end of the lake.

A superb 18-hole PGA golf course designed by Robert Trent Jones is not only one of the most challenging in the United States but certainly one of the most beautiful. Its greens and fairways are laced with icy mountain brooks. On them or high above them on the Mount Rose highway they appear to be a necklace of gem-like mountain meadows.

In the winter of 1967 Arthur Wood and his executive vice-president, Harold Tiller, opened Ski Incline, the region's newest and most exciting ski resort. Virtually independent of the weather, Ski Incline's many runs are guaranteed perfect snow by means of an elaborate system of sprays that can put down a three foot base overnight. On runs supplemented by ample natural snow that is mechanically "groomed" each morning families can enjoy everything from nursery slopes to expert trails from late autumn to late spring. Or they can sun themselves on the largest ski veranda in the country and watch fellow enthusiasts moving up Ski Incline's five modern lifts.

Needless to say, major capital investments such as this have done much to increase the value of land already purchased in the area. Easily accessible from San Francisco and Los Angeles over major highways and freeways, Incline Village is rapidly becoming the finest all-year mountain community in the West. (We make no bones about it. We liked what we saw so well that we invested there!)

Another area that seems to offer a fine investment opportunity is Mammoth Mountain, south of Lake Tahoe, in the same Sierra Nevada range. Here again the vision and energy of one man is responsible for a major miracle.

The man is fifty-two-year-old Dave McCoy of Los Angeles. Once a hydrographer for the Los Angeles Department of Water and Power, McCoy skied over the high watershed measuring the snowfall so vital to Southern California's water needs. The perfect skiing conditions and the breath-taking beauty of the Mammoth Mountain region "hooked" Dave McCoy. Using his intimate firsthand knowledge of the best locations, he began thirty years ago with a modest rope tow operation. Today six chair lifts, two T-bars and a spectacular million-dollar gondola handle upward of 4000 skiers a day during the season—and with remarkably little waiting. Ninety per cent of the skiers come from Greater Los Angeles. The remainder are from the San Francisco Bay area and out-of-state visitors.

Inevitably Dave McCoy's money magnets (his ski facilities) have attracted other investors. Restaurants, hotels, motels and related service businesses have created a booming community at Mammoth Lakes. Long a summer campers' paradise, this area too is becoming an all-year playground.

As a natural result residential developments are appearing. Most impressive in the area is Mammoth Slopes, a 140 acre master-planned community within minutes of the major ski installations. Boasting sewers, underground electric and telephone lines and well-paved county roads and streets, Mammoth Slopes property seems certain to benefit from Dave McCoy's activities by attracting buyers who will want to build combination summer homes and ski lodges. Building has already begun. If the developers continue as they are there can be little doubt about a substantial increase in the value of property purchased during the early stages of Mammoth Slopes development.

Through the efforts of such organizations as the Antelope Valley Board of Trade and the highly aggressive Mojave Industrial Action Committee who have already attracted $300 million in heavy industry, there is little reason to believe that it won't happen sooner than many expect. With the recent incorporation of the City of Palmdale another powerful force for development has come to the valley, a force receiving dynamic impetus from the first new railroad in the U.S.A. in forty years, the Southern Pacific's Colton-Palmdale Cutoff, and the impending incorporation of the Army's huge Plant 42 super-sonic air facility into the Los Angeles Metropolitan Airport complex.

Two other developers should be noted in these pages as examples of daring and enterprise not unmixed with genius. One is named Nathan K. Mendelsohn. Mr. Mendelsohn's most obvious claim to fame is that he is presently in the midst of building two of the largest, new, complete city-communities in the world, the 82,000-acre California City project at the apex of the Emerald Triangle in Southern California's Antelope Valley and an equally impressive community known as Colorado City not far from Pueblo, Colorado.

It is not hard to find skeptics who will try to convince you that Nat Mendelsohn is a bit land-daffy, that he must be to visualize in the middle of a desert valley a complete city with man-made lakes, golf courses, artificial hills in "Central Park" from which gush artificial falls of very real water, of which he apparently has an indigenous abundance! And still, Mendelsohn has built them, and is building more, and people, tired of the congested streets and the even more congested air of the metropolitan Los Angeles area, are happily buying in his smog-free, high desert development with its three hundred guaranteed days of sunshine each year.

"When the people outnumber the jack rabbits, I'll believe it!" commented one native of Mojave, the nearest sizable town and a booming new, heavy industrial center itself. But if you'll look at the series of progress photos printed in this book you'll see that Mr. Mendelsohn and his staff appear to have the jack rabbits on the run indeed.

What this former professor of sociology from Columbia University in New York City is counting on is the meticulous research his organization had done on the Antelope Valley area *before* an acre of land was purchased. Like the late Fred Allen's "well-rehearsed ad lib," the well-planned miracle is the one most apt to happen. Nat Mendelsohn is con-

vinced from his own research that the great Pacific Coast
strip city will eventually engulf California City. So are the
people who bought there.

The Bass development is called Apple Valley. It is situated
in California's San Bernardino County a few miles southeast
of the thriving railroad and agricultural center, Victorville.

Apple Valley as conceived by Mr. Bass and his planners
is to be a complete community. While its temperate all-year
climate will inevitably weigh the scales in favor of resort
activities, plans call for a cross section of enterprises ranging
from agriculture to light industry. The area lies at three thousand feet, is generally ten degrees cooler than the low desert
area during any given season and, unlike some desert areas,
it has an abundance of indigenous water. Its mutual water
system is a model one.

There are the usual amenities, a PGA golf course and extremely well done country club, The Apple Valley Inn and
guest ranch recently leased by film actor Roy Rogers' Frontier Hotels Incorporated, a Western museum containing
mostly Roy Rogers-Dale Evans memorabilia, the Roy Rogers
home ranch used mainly for breeding thoroughbred horses,
large administration buildings for the recently merged Bass-
Reserve Oil and Gas Corporation interests whose headquar-
ters have been moved to Apple Valley from San Francisco,
extensive business establishments, five grammar schools, one
junior high school and a new four-year high school.

Once thought of as being "remote" from the dense population centers, new freeways have become grasping tentacles
of the growing Southern California "megaloctopus" and over
them flow an ever increasing stream of persons seeking more
clean air, more elbow room, more home for their money,
more opportunities to enjoy free time. Apple Valley lies adjacent to two major interstate arteries, US 40 and US 15 and
is within easy driving distance of several major Southern
California mountain resorts including both Lake Arrowhead
and Big Bear Lake.

Newton Bass, unlike most of his contemporaries, does not advertise extensively.

"We have never advertised a lot for sale here," he told us. "We prefer to let satisfied buyers tell their friends about Apple Valley. We think it makes for a tighter knit group with common interests although we certainly do not discourage folks who just happen in."

Roy Rogers has initiated an extensive advertising campaign to attract guests to the Apple Valley Inn. Inevitably this will produce business from those who come and like what they see. But after our conversations with Mr. Bass we did not get the impression that the emphasis would be on lower income appeal, at least so far as potential permanent residents are concerned.

Now, let's meet one last type of "promoter" who adds tremendous value to land. Two such men here in the West are Walt Disney, with his truly incomparable Disneyland, and Walter Knott, who grew from tenant farmer and roadside fruit-stand operator into the creator of the equally amazing 200-acre Knott's Berry Farm, not far from Disneyland.

So much has been written and broadcast about Walt Disney that we won't even attempt to cover him here. Walt is just a fact of our lives. And because of him not only the West but the world is often a happier place to live in.

Walter Knott's story is a combination of Horatio Alger and Jeeter Lester. The last thing in the world he'd claim to be is a land developer or promoter or for that matter anything but a dedicated American with a certain amount of business sense and enterprise. And still it is true that anyone who does anything that attracts favorable attention in an area and tends to increase land values is, in the best sense, a land developer and promoter. Walter and Cordelia Knott and their remarkable family have certainly done much for Buena Park, since they first became tenant farmers on 10 acres of land there in 1920.

Since then well over 20 million persons have visited the

exciting and sentimental monument to grass roots Americanism with its famous ghost town, its historic narrow-gauge railroad, its frontier theater, its wagon camp and country church, its placer mine where kids of all ages can pan a smidgin of real gold, and its incredibly successful restaurants, which have served well over one and three-quarter million dinners each year for the past several years.

In 1934, three years after Walter and Cordelia Knott had scraped to purchase their first and second 10-acre parcels of farmland and try it on their own instead of as tenant farmers, we drove our old Chevy down to Buena Park on a Sunday and dined on home-fried chicken and boysenberry pie. We can remember well how little we paid for those dinners in that modest little shack. It was 65 cents each! And we remember equally well that the dinners were delicious!

When we asked Walter Knott what he had paid for that land he replied, "I bought the first 10 acres in 1927 from the man I farmed it for. The price then was $1500 an acre."

We asked him to estimate what the land was worth today.

"Oh," he mused, "I guess the average price would be $25,000 an acre—for just the land, I mean. We did sell some of it to a bank and two savings and loan companies not long ago. That went for $1000 a front foot."

He remembered something else then and a web of smile wrinkles grew at the corners of his eyes. (Walter Knott has the eyes of a pioneer who has beheld a great vision and has seen it come true.) "About ten years ago," he said, "Mother and I had a chance to buy that 40-acre piece across the street. It was in oranges then and the man wanted $3500 an acre. Well, we figured that a grove like that couldn't pay out and it would be too costly to grub out the trees and farm it so we let it go."

We couldn't resist a question. "What happened to it?" we asked.

"Oh, it's still there," he replied. "Trouble is, the fellow wants $20,000 an acre for it now!"

After the soft whistles of wonderment we asked Mr. Knott how he felt about letting the land get away from him.

"Well," he said thoughtfully, "we have made it a practice to buy only the land we need. If we had felt like buying land for speculation we could have been rich folks by now. But we have plowed back most of the profit we've made into improving this place and making sure that we can continue to serve our customers. To succeed, you must serve. We try to serve not only our customers, but our employees too. We feel that is a basic obligation under our wonderful system of free enterprise in this country. We've been so busy doing that we haven't had time for land speculation as such."

As developers and as citizens, the Knott family has not only served its customers and its employees (nearly a thousand of them) but it has served the community of Buena Park and the entire country as well.

While it is undoubtedly true that all of these western communities would have grown under the impetus of *people pressure,* there can be little argument that the ones which have grown most rapidly and solidly are those in which exceptional developers in every category, in all of our states, have built something substantial and have provided a genuine service. If one fills a need, one provides a service.

The needs of an exploding population are manifold. But certainly, in the long run, none is greater than the need for a good piece of land. Often, as was the case with Walter and Cordelia Knott, that land may not be yours in the beginning. But if you are determined to put your roots down, one of the first things to do, after securing your economy, is to try to get title to a place of your own. For us Americans that is not only one of our greatest privileges, it can also be one of our greatest adventures.

"Owning a piece of land gives a man a different feel about his country!" said Walter Knott.

To that we can only add, "Amen!"

ACKNOWLEDGMENTS

As we have made clear in the introduction, our blueprint for finding a good investment or speculation is intended for use by "average investors" like ourselves. It is largely the result of analyzing and interpreting our own experience over the past decade or so.

In the opening chapter we have made note of the very great debt of gratitude we owe the members of the Stein family of Sayville, Long Island. That debt is owed equally to Captain Kenneth Stein and his wife, Eunice; Capt. Fred Stein, Jr. and his wife, Garnet; and to Capt. and Mrs. Fred Stein, Sr. Quite as much as their wise counsel, their warm friendship and unstinting hospitality made us want to put our roots down near them in Suffolk County, New York, and later in Martin County, Florida.

Throughout this book we have mentioned the names of many of the helpful persons to whom we have had occasion to turn in order to corroborate facts about western land as an investment. Our gratitude to them is implicit in the use of their quotations and in the use of the material provided by them.

But we want to add a special thanks to Commissioner Milton G. Gordon of California, Division of Real Estate, and to the assistant commissioner for Southern California, Gerald E. Harrington, for making available to us the studies prepared by the Real Estate Research Program, Graduate School of Business Administration and by the School of Law of the University of California, Los Angeles.

The two studies were prepared for the National Conference of Interstate Land Sales held in San Francisco on October 1, 1962.

We first came across them in the office of Gerald J. McBride, executive secretary of the Nevada Real Estate Commission. Mr. McBride predicted that the studies would become the basis for the new state laws needed to control the spreading abuses in the promotion and sales of tens of thousands of acres of raw land in some of the most remote areas of our western states.

Although many of the legal philosophies propounded in the study were "over the heads" of amateur land investors such as we, we were reassured to find that our own research was confirmed by the first part of the study which dealt with the history and the growth cycles of land developments in the United States.

We do not pretend that any of the material provided by any source other than the editorial staff of *U.S. News & World Report* pertains to or purports to support "The Strip City Theory," which is the basis for our own land-finding formula. We had come to this theory independently some years back but had not given it a name. The growth patterns in the nation which in the end determined the logical label, "strip cities," became obvious to us after our research had made the discovery of their presence inevitable. But it remained for *U.S. News & World Report* to set them forth graphically in their remarkable study in the September 18, 1961, issue of the magazine. We are grateful to the editorial staff of *U.S. News & World Report* for permitting us to refer to their study and use certain materials from it. The strip-city charts in Chapter Five are *not* actual reproductions of their original detailed maps. Rather, they are simplified charts based on the originals. To them we have added certain "islands" of growth which had become apparent to us from our own travels and research. They are general designations and pretend none of the accuracy of detail of the original strip-city maps upon which our adaptations have been superimposed.

In any attempt to predict the future growth of our country there must be a certain element of speculation. Time may confirm the accuracy of some of the predictions and disprove others. None of the material herein provided by *any* source is represented as being used solely to support our personal interpretation and projections of our country's growth patterns. Neither do we imply that those generous persons and organizations who have contributed material to this book endorse its contents in whole or in part.

Human nature being what it is we suppose that those who advocate extremely stringent laws to control land promotion will think we have been "too easy" on land promoters in general. On the other hand, we imagine those promoters who deem *any* government interference with their business practices an invasion of their right to compete under the free enterprise system will feel that we have been "too hard" on them.

However that may be, we wish to remind both groups that nothing in this book is to be construed as an attempt to sit in judgment of them or to prejudice them with the readers. Those land promoters whose activities have come under state and federal scrutiny will be indicted by their own practices and publicly judged by due process of law.

In addition to those already mentioned we wish to thank (in alphabetical order but not necessarily in the order of the importance of their contributions) the following old and new friends:

Jack Abrams, commissioner, Okanogan County, Washington, for his observations on the future of the Methow Valley upon completion of the incredible North Cross-State Highway;

E. H. Azbill of the Salt Lake City Chamber of Commerce;

William I. Barris, assistant to the president, Apple Valley Development Company;

Richard Blalock, vice president of the Crystalaire Country Club and the adjoining development at Llano in the Emerald Triangle area of Southern California's Antelope Valley;

Paul R. Brown, executive secretary of the New Mexico Real Estate Commission, who provided us with up to the minute data about his state's remarkable growth and a copy, still wet from the presses, of New Mexico's effective new subdivision law;

Chauncey T. Burgess, Jr. of Red Bluff, California, who as county assessor of Tehama County (and a boyhood friend whose father inspired the character "Chauncy Parsons" in the current novel *The Richest Poor Folks*) gave us a most objective look at the increases in land values in northern California;

Richard A. Bittman, acting director of the Department of Development, State of New Mexico;

Robert A. Byers, chairman of the Mojave Industrial Action

Committee, for the detailed explanation of the activities of that
aggressive group and its marked effect upon the industrial growth
of the Antelope Valley;

D. James Cannon, director, Utah Tourist and Publicity Council,
Salt Lake City, for his help in coordinating information on his
state;

Harold E. Coward, vice president of the Bank of America,
Laguna Beach, California, for his help in researching that far-
flung banking empire—the largest private bank in the world—
whose own growth is a dramatic chapter in the growth of California;

Audrey L. Forbes, manager of Reader Service of *U.S. News &
World Report,* Washington, D.C., for the most prompt and courteous help in securing the material on "The Strip City Theory";

Governor Paul Fannin of Arizona for the time he granted us in
his heavy schedule and for the cooperation of the Arizona Real
Estate Commission and the Arizona Development Board, who
really bore the brunt of getting us properly informed about that
exploding state;

Thomas Jardine, public relations manager of *The Valley Times*
TODAY, North Hollywood, California for opening that historic
paper's archives;

John E. Hempel, assistant commissioner, State of California
Department of Real Estate, for his assistance in coordinating
information and appointments;

Mrs. "Van" Hoosten of the Riverside Chamber of Commerce
for help in getting Fred Bauman's extraordinary shots of that
city;

Fred Layman, assistant real estate commissioner of the State
of Oregon, for his courtesy when we dropped in "out of the blue"
for a discussion of eastern and central Oregon subdivisions, and
for taking the trouble to "get us together" with Commissioner
Robert J. Jensen, whose help is noted elsewhere in this book;

Jack Lehman, manager of the Nevada State Development
Board, for reams of excellent material on his state;

Joseph J. LaBarbera, director of advertising and publicity for
Title Insurance and Trust Company, Los Angeles, for his coopera-

tion in providing literally scores of research sources from which we have quoted liberally, with his permission;

William O. Mager, secretary of the California Land Title Association for permission to use historical material and figures from promotional booklets published by his group;

Walter J. Miller, assistant commissioner for education and publications, California Real Estate Commission, for his help in obtaining the bound copy of the U.C.L.A. report on legal and economic aspects of interstate land sales so useful in confirming much of the material herein;

Erwin E. Mochel, realtor and president of the Antelope Valley Realty Board, whose assistance was invaluable in obtaining an accurate picture of that area's incredible growth;

Chris Metos of the Utah State Department of Highways for his help;

J. Edward Murray, managing editor of *The Arizona Republic,* for his cooperation in aiding us to get a well-rounded point of view on the problem of remote subdivisions in the West;

Cedric Olson, manager of the Chamber of Commerce, Las Vegas, Nevada, for the valuable material provided which enabled us to understand the spectacular growth pattern of that area;

L. E. "Pat" Patrick, realtor and president of the Palmdale Realty Board in the Antelope Valley, for his lucid and enthusiastic picture of the growth of his particular part of the Emerald Triangle area;

C. V. Paul, president of Antelope Valley's Crystalaire Country Club, who gave us our most detailed instruction in the complexities of starting a first-class development which involves, among other things, not only homesites, golf courses, lakes, and other recreational facilities (as do many other western developments) but also the creation of a bona fide public utility to provide unlimited water for the area. Our appreciation also to his charming wife, Lorena Paul, a true western pioneer daughter, whose own efforts have had much to do with the success of Crystalaire;

Clifford L. Rawson, executive director of the Antelope Valley Progress Association, whose tireless help in calling meetings, assembling material, providing photos and patient counsel in compiling the facts on the Antelope Valley's past, present, and fabulously promising future, did so much to make the researching of this book a memorable adventure;

Maggie Savoy, woman's editor, *The Arizona Republic*, for so many kindnesses above and beyond the call of duty. (Gals with Maggie's enthusiasm can spoil authors "rotten!" And we love it!)

Clyde L. Simpson, assistant vice president, Security First National Bank, Los Angeles, who opened both his archives and remarkable memory to us and did much to help us get a realistic perspective on California's growth during the past three decades;

Milton Stark, district information officer, State of California Department of Public Works, Division of Highways, District VII, for a minute examination of the concrete and asphalt tentacles of our California "megaloctopuses";

Eileen Trainer, custodian of the Collection of Historical Photographs of the Title Insurance and Trust Company, Los Angeles, for her patience and invaluable assistance in going through hundreds of photos to find those most applicable to this book;

William E. Warne, director, California State Department of Water Resources, for a generous and enlightening interview on one of the West's most pressing problems, the equitable distribution of its water;

Carroll R. West, vice president and manager of the Public Relations Dept., Title Insurance and Trust Company;

Richard Winn, public information officer, Department of Water Resources, State of California, for his patience and persistence in getting the facts to us and in opening doors for important interviews;

James A. Wood, publisher of the *Advance-Star* and *Green Sheet*, Burlingame, California, for his painstaking research and the photos from that paper's archives—and to "Jim," too, for so many past favors where books are concerned;

Alan J. Williams, senior public relations representative, the Metropolitan Water District of Southern California, for the research material and the thorough explanation of the vast complexities of providing for present needs and anticipating future needs in an area whose rate of growth exceeds that of any community thus far known.

We have tried to be meticulous in keeping tabs on the names of those who have been helpful but we'd be more than mere mortals if we find we've gone through these acknowledgments without some inadvertent omissions. To those then, whose contributions were deeply appreciated but not noted here, our apologies and reassurances of lasting gratitude.

In this revised edition we must acknowledge the help of still more interested persons.

Among these, valuable assistance came from E. D. Ettinger, Director of Public Relations, Rancho California; Derrill Trenholm of Beveridge, Penny & Bennett, Incorporated, Los Angeles; Frank Davis, Vice-President, Colorado City Development Company; Penn Thayer, Vice-President, M. Penn Phillips Company; Francis Sinclair, Crystal Bay Development Company, Gene Voght of the Holly Corporation; Park Hinkson, Mammoth Slopes and Tom Johnston, Director of Public Relations for the Mammoth Ski Area. There were others too—the patient and efficient secretaries who "followed through"—and the junior executives who often got stuck with the "dirty work" of showing us around and coming up with the answers to scores of questions, not all of them "polite." Among these young men—and for service well above and beyond the call of duty—we wish to thank Newell Stickler, Executive Assistant, Rancho California. One can ask a lot of questions about an 87,500 acre development!

L.F.C.
L.M.C.

SUPPLEMENT

Unfortunately, as the deadline for the revised material in this new edition of *The Simple Truth about Western Land Investment* approached we still had not received from the State of Hawaii's Real Estate Commission the material promised when we visited there in January of 1967 to take a firsthand look at investment possibilities.

We are at a loss to understand this delay since Mr. Robert E. Bekeart, Executive Secretary of the Hawaiian Real Estate Commission, was most cordial and cooperative when we visited with him. Indeed, he spent several hours going over the commission's files, showing us the problems the commission faces with land promotions in the islands, showed us concrete evidence of effective policing of unscrupulous and marginal promoters and discussed the need for and nature of new legislation that would permit the state more effective control. In addition, Mr. Bekeart promised us photographs of both desirable and undesirable subdivisions most of which seemed to be on the big island of Hawaii.

Hardly a person on the mainland has not seen the colorful advertising placed by land promoters who have parcels of "paradise" to sell in our newest and most colorful state. Thousands of persons have bought, sight unseen. Here again, these buyers have made a fundamental mistake.

While not all of this land is "worthless" by any means, (some of it is better than advertised), the major portion of the subdivided fee simple land could have problems attached to its purchase.

In more than one instance the subdividers have not kept up their "paved streets." Mr. Bekeart showed us photographs of some such streets along which the commissioners were forced to hack their way with machetes in order to find the signs, so quickly had the jungle taken over. In a number of places signs reading SITE

OF PROPOSED CLUB HOUSE and other very iffy money magnets were literally strangled in the tangle of lush tropical growth on the windward (wet!) side of the island and rains had all but obliterated the thin macadam roads.

Several of the subdivisions were laid out on what geologists call "technically hot" lava flows, a flow needing a minimum of forty years to cool through. That does not mean that a buyer would get a huge hot foot while visiting his property. On the contrary, his land may be grown over with a matted tangle of vines. But technically the flow of lava is still "warm" at its base and therefore subject to movement, stresses and probably cracking.

In one subdivision where cesspools were required by ordinance the cost of drilling through the lava cap was estimated to be at least twice the cost of the land itself. Water was a problem. Power was not near, neither were telephones nor gas. And there seemed little likelihood that these utilities would be brought in since absentee owners, mostly from the mainland, had bought the land as a speculation and only a handful of the several thousand lots sold were being built upon, not enough population to handle the bond issues necessary to bring in these civilized amenities.

Only near Hilo did we see fee simple subdivisions that appeared to be growing and these were modest indeed by mainland standards.

The problem is not a lack of splendid land in the islands. On the contrary. But the best of it, millions of acres of it, are owned outright or controlled by a relatively few large families or corporations or Huis (Chinese family syndicates).

Consequently, the fee simple land that is available is apt to be the least desirable in the islands. Except for urban lots and some small farms, private ownership by the average citizen is limited. And this accounts for a curious phenomenon: Most Hawaiians who wish to buy land do so on the mainland.

One broker dealing in California land told us that his firm had sold 24,000 parcels of desert land to Hawaiians, mostly of oriental extraction, so great is the urge of the small Hawaiian worker to own, in fee simple, a piece of the United States that he and his family can truly call their own. In short, Hawaiian land is generally out of reach of the average Hawaiian. One Hawaiian-Japanese family told us that the land they could afford to buy would not support crops sufficient for their own personal needs much less provide a marketable surplus.

As with the mainland, the sight-unseen buyer who succumbs to the four-color blandishments of the land promoter or developer, the native Hawaiian who buys "stateside" land sight unseen, is apt to suffer buyers' remorse if he ever comes to the mainland to see it and try to live on it.

We have seen some of that land and it would qualify for the very heart of that arid, undeveloped (but not necessarily undevelopable) Western land that we call, "West Hellangone."

Those Islanders who have bought in such developments as California City will have spent their money well, in our opinion, *if* they do come "stateside" and make use of the land . . . *and if they have bought large enough parcels to make a minimum economic agricultural unit.*

We asked one Hawaiian buyer if he had ever been to California to see his land.

"No," he replied. "The family saved the money and we pooled it like the Chinese do. When we had enough money to buy, we did."

When we suggested that he was taking a big chance with his life savings he replied, "What other chance do we have?"

Our answer seemed to give him pause.

"Why," we asked, "didn't the family pool about $250 and send you over for two or three days to look at the land first?"

He was a long time answering.

"Well—we didn't think about that. We've never been off the islands—and besides—the salesman said we had to make up our mind in twenty-four hours or the land would be gone."

We told him that if he had gone to the real estate commission and made inquiry, in all probability the salesman would have been gone in twenty-four hours too!

Promoters, understanding the almost psychotic anxiety that many natives have to own something that will give them security in their old age, have exploited this fear, often shamelessly. But then, that is not necessarily an insular evil, we've seen them do it on the mainland too.

To sum up Hawaii for the average small investor: It is a delightful place to visit, to vacation, and in some cases to work. But as a place to make a sound investment in real estate, it is no place for the small investor. In fact, we were told that it took quite a bit of doing for a Rockefeller to get control (mostly via lease) of enough land to build a sumptuous new resort hotel on Hawaii's Kona Coast.

Again—Caveat Emptor! Buyer Beware! If you are hell-bent to own a parcel of heavenly Hawaii, spend a few hundred dollars and fly down for a look first. And before you buy ask those *Thirteen Lucky Questions* set down on page 66. Then, when you've got the answers, double-check them with the real estate commission in Honolulu, for the State of Hawaii, like California, is also a state of mind—and in the face of all the beatific ballyhoo and real estate razzle-dazzle you may be swayed as easily as a Waikiki palm—and too late, find yourself *PAA* and your bankroll *PAU!*

Since the first edition of this book came out in 1964 we have had literally hundreds of letters from readers asking us to counsel them on land purchases.

It is very flattering to be judged such an expert. But we would like to say here that our own ethics, and the law as well, preclude that possibility.

The male half of this collaboration is primarily a novelist. We have undertaken two non-fiction books as warnings to friends who have been cheated both in land dealings and in the selection of a retirement home (See *The Retirement Trap*, Doubleday, 1965). It does not seem likely that we will undertake any more nonfiction—unless, of course, we get sufficiently exercised about some new abuse.

Also, we have been asked to opine about a number of western communities and their potential for successful investment.

We are reluctant to attempt such analysis; but we will make herewith—and briefly—some general observations about one or two of the areas concerning which we've received inquiries.

PALM SPRINGS: This is primarily a wintering area and a delightful place, perhaps the most dramatic geographically and climatically in the west. It is literally possible during the winter to laze around your swimming pool and watch the skiers atop Mount San Gorgonio some 13,000 feet above you. If you wish to join them, a five or ten minute drive to the spectacular tramway will take you from 80 degree temperatures to below freezing. And within several hours you can be back down to the desert again for a pre-supper dip in your pool. The same goes for summer; except for skiing.

As for investment opportunities—they are very good indeed—but considerable capital will be required to make it big. Except for small building lots and some business locations in the outlying districts, the day has passed for the small investor to make a killing there. By small investor, we mean the person who buys a lot or 2½ acres in undeveloped subdivisions for a few hundred dollars down and say, $30 a month including interest and principal.

There are some good inexpensive buys in the general area of Palm Springs however and several new communities are growing up—sort of satellite communities—taking their advantage from the hundreds of millions that have been invested in Palm Springs in the past three decades. But reflected glory may not necessarily mean reflected profits. Ask those thirteen questions again!

FLORIDA: In the body of the book we indicated that we had made some modest investments in Florida. Many letters came from residents of that lovely state, and from northern states, asking us for opinions about the best investment localities. To them we have replied by referring to the contents of this book for the formula for locating the most likely areas of progress are all in these pages.

Since the first edition was published, the late Walt Disney and his organization, have begun construction on a fantastic new recreation area near Orlando. If the history of the area around the original Disneyland in Anaheim, California, carries within it any lessons, then for some years to come there will be wonderful investment possibilities in the Orlando area. But be forewarned—the time to have made those investments at bargain prices was well *before* the announcement of the larger development. Now, while opportunity undoubtedly exists, it is apt to be advantageous only for the large, sophisticated investor with capital and know-how. As we keep pointing out, the trick is to predict the path of progress by research and then invest there early and hold on. It is even better to make use of the land yourself to help stimulate progress. But again, that requires capital.

We have chosen the Stuart-Rio-Jensen Beach area north of Palm Beach, Florida, for our eastern investment because of the truly remarkable all-year vacation and business opportunities there. The Stuart inlet, as we have indicated earlier, is the key to the development of the area as a vacationland. It may very well be the key to far more important development too since there is a fine deep-water harbor potential there too.

We subscribe to the Stuart *News* and keep abreast of progress there. Lately we have seen hopeful signs that the government will help Martin County with funds to stabilize the Stuart inlet. If and when that happens it is reasonable to look for a spectacular upswing in values in the entire area. That is what we are count-ing on. And even though it may take more time than we ex-pected, we intend to enjoy the area as part-time residents for there is no finer salt and fresh water fishing in the world than the gulf stream and the north and south forks of the St. Lucie River. (We still dream about the sailfish we took there—and the snook that fought like tarpon!) And if one wants to fish the Gulf of Mexico, one has only to enter the St. Lucie Canal, traverse the locks, cross Lake Okeechobee, navigate the western end of the canal and come out on the opposite coast at Fort Myers. Or, by inland waterway, you can go all the way north to New York and New Jersey—with a couple of brief runs "outside."

In closing we want to thank all those who have written express-ing their gratitude for the information we have tried to convey in this book. And we wish to thank those who have provided us with new information to update it. And we want to warn readers again that there is no "Royal Road to Riches" in land. Research is needed and research takes work. But, if you make an adventure of it as we have done, it can be rewarding in more ways than one!